GOOD COOKING WITH WINE

Mary Reynolds

HAMLYN
London · New York · Sydney · Toronto

Acknowledgements

The following colour photographs are by courtesy of:
Fruit Producers' Council
Apples flamed with rum, page 59
Uncle Ben's Rice
Chicken Marengo, page 23

Jacket picture by courtesy of Grants of St. James's
Front cover, Coq au vin rouge (see page 36)
Back cover, Crêpes suzette (see page 9)
Dishes kindly loaned by Harvey Nichols and Company,
Knightsbridge, London

Photograph by John Lee

Illustrated by Ian Garrard

First published in the Leisure Plan series in 1970
by The Hamlyn Publishing Group Limited,
London · New York · Sydney · Toronto
Hamlyn House, Feltham, Middlesex, England

Second edition 1973
© Copyright The Hamlyn Publishing Group Limited 1973

ISBN 0 600 33919 X

Printed in England by Chapel River Press, Andover

Contents

Introduction

About cooking with wine

Whether you drink it or cook with it, wine immeasurably enhances the flavour of food. In cooking it makes a difference out of all proportion to the modest amounts generally used.

There is no mystique about cooking with wine – it is simply an ingredient with a special ability to round out the flavour of a dish, adding a richness, mellowness or fillip. Naturally you do not add wine willy nilly to any and every recipe but only where it harmonises with the other ingredients.

The basic point to remember about cooking with table wine is that you must cook it sufficiently to evaporate the alcohol and allow the flavour to mellow. Taste the gravy of a wine casserole some time after preparing and again after several hours gentle simmering and you will see exactly what I mean. It does not follow that all wine recipes have to be cooked for hours. On the contrary – but in quick cooking dishes invariably you will be instructed to '. . . add the wine and bubble briskly for several minutes . . .' which is another way of driving off the alcohol and concentrating and mellowing the wine essences. In fact, when you have time, it is never a mistake to reduce a wine by rapid boiling before using it for cooking. Try this when you want to make a really superb Coq au vin rouge.

Cooking with wine is essentially an art rather than a science and, as with painting, you must be prepared to experiment. Wines themselves vary greatly in character and strength, and the golden rule is *'It's better to add too little than too much'*. This is especially true of spirits and liqueurs which entirely lose their charm if overdone. When you do not have exactly what the recipe stipulates in stock try improvising with what is available. Except in fish and shellfish recipes, white and red wine is often interchangeable. Diluted dry vermouth can stand in for white wine in fish and poultry recipes, and sherry for Madeira or Marsala. The flavour of the resulting dish will be changed, of course – but you might make a gastronomic discovery – who knows?

Suggestions about the kinds of wine most suited to different foods are given in the introduction to each chapter, where you will also find notes on relevant techniques such as flaming, marinating and basting. The notes on 'Wines, spirits and liqueurs' are a brief guide to the types most generally useful for adding a gourmet touch to your dishes.

Wines, spirits and liqueurs

When you cook with wines or spirits the alcohol is mostly evaporated and what remains to enhance the dish is the basic essence and quality. So be sure the wines and spirits are sound and of reasonable quality.

Table wines

These are the wines you drink with food and, generally speaking, any medium dry wine you enjoy drinking will be fine for cooking. It would be very extravagant to use a vintage wine, unless it has gone past its prime and needs using up. But you will be disappointed with the cooked dish if you use a thin, excessively dry or a too cheap wine which lacks body and flavour. Never use a sour or acid wine (such as you might have if the cork is not replaced in a bottle in storage), its only use is as wine vinegar.

If you drink wine regularly you may not need to buy any specially for cooking because the 'heels' left in the bottles may be sufficient. Alternatively if you are having an ordinary red wine with your meal it improves if opened a couple of hours beforehand which enables you to pour off a little for cooking. Otherwise keep a half bottle or two of both red and white wine in stock for cooking.

Red wine

Choose a young, strong and full bodied wine. For example a Beaujolais, Mâcon or St. Emilion, a Chianti or Barbaresco, or a wine with similar qualities.

White wine

Choose a strong, medium dry wine such as a Mâcon, Graves, Entre-Deux-Mers or similar. A really dry wine can be unpleasantly acid when cooked. Sweet wines come into their own for syllabubs, fresh peaches in wine, and puddings generally.

Fruit wines and home-made wines

Provided they have the general characteristics outlined above, any and all of these wines are good for cooking. They will vary considerably in character so be prepared to experiment, and adapt recipes to suit the ingredients.

Fortified wines

These are the wines you normally drink before or after, rather than with, a meal. They have been strengthened with brandy and have in consequence a higher proof spirit and more concentrated flavour. They range from the very dry to the sweet and luscious, and have many, many uses in the kitchen.

Sherry blends happily with any number of different foods and has a unique place in the kitchen. It does not matter in the least whether it comes from Spain, Australia, South Africa or Cyprus provided it has good body and flavour. Use a medium dry sherry for soups, sauces and poultry dishes, and the same or a sweeter sherry for trifles and sweets.

Madeira gives a wonderful flavour-fillip to consommés if added at the last moment before serving. An essential ingredient of Madeira sauce, and excellent for kidney and veal dishes, use it for sweet dishes too. A medium dry Madeira (Sercial or Verdelho) is the most useful.

Port is excellent for poultry and game dishes, and for many sweets. Use a medium dry tawny port for savoury dishes, and an inexpensive 'port type' or 'rich ruby' wine for sweet dishes.

Marsala is the sweet brown Sicilian wine that features in Italian recipes. Use it for soups and sauces, with chicken livers, with ham, and especially in Zabaglione. It varies in strength and sweetness so taste as you cook rather than follow recipes implicitly. Bottles labelled 'Cooking Marsala' contain wine of lower proof spirit and are cheaper.

Vermouths and other aperitif wines

Vermouth is a blend of wines to which some spirit and a variety of 'extras' are added. It has a higher alcohol content that most table wines but is less strong than the traditional fortified wines. The extras vary but usually consist of roots, tree barks, herbs, fruit rinds, berries, and lastly wormwood which gives the typical slightly bitter taste. Sweet vermouths are interesting flavourings for sweet dishes such as cakes, creams and desserts; and, added to a very dry wine they can 'round out' the flavour of fish and savoury dishes. Dry vermouth, especially the French, is ideal for fish and meat dishes, or any savoury recipe in which both wine and herbs are used. Because vermouth is stronger than table wine use a little less.

Other aperitif wines can be used in the kitchen according to personal taste. Devotees of Pernod, for instance, consider it a good flavour for fish dishes.

Liqueurs

The majority of liqueurs are made of grape spirit to which sugar and syrup flavourings, particularly fruit, spices and herbs, have been added. Most are sweet and rich, although a few, notably Kirsch and Calvados, are dry. They vary in strength, and some are made in different strengths for different countries.

The highly concentrated flavour of liqueurs adds

excitement to hot soufflés, ices, sorbets, desserts and gâteaux. You will find many ideas in the relevant chapters in this book. Miniature bottles containing 2 to 2½ tablespoonfuls are invaluable for experimenting. If asked to select six for the kitchen from the dozens available I would choose:

a One of the orange-flavoured liqueurs – either Grand Marnier, Cointreau, Curacao, or Aurum (orange and bergamot-flavoured Italian liqueur).

b Kirsch – a colourless liqueur made from bitter cherries with a wonderful flavour affinity for various fruits, for cream fillings and ice cream. Buy the genuine fruit alcohol labelled Kirschwasser.

c One of the aromatic herb-flavoured liqueurs – Green Chartreuse, Bénédictine or Strega.

d Apricot brandy.

e Tia Maria (coffee).

f Crème de Noyau (almond) or Crème de Menthe (peppermint).

Spirits

All spirits are expensive, but the majority of recipes need only a spoonful or two to give them distinction. A duty-free bottle can be brought home from trips abroad, and half or quarter size bottles are available, and even miniatures.

Brandy is distilled from wine and has a special affinity with food. Without doubt the most generally useful spirit in the kitchen and used as a preservative as well as a flavouring, and for flaming (see 'All about flaming' page 7). Although it is wasteful to use a liqueur brandy in the kitchen, you will be wise to choose a sound brand – a good South African, Australian or Cyprus brandy or a Three Star French Cognac. When travelling in France you may be able to buy quite cheaply a good local marc (made from the residue of pressed grapes instead of from wine), or an Eau de Vie, such as French housewives use.

Rum is a wonderful flavour for puddings, desserts and cakes, and excellent for flaming. Of the various types, for cooking choose golden Jamaican rum, which has the fullest flavour.

Whisky has a limited use in the kitchen but is increasingly employed as a flavouring and for flaming. Either Scotch or Irish whisky (the latter is usually spelt with an 'e') can be used, Irish having a more pronounced flavour.

Cider

This native English 'wine' is an excellent, inexpensive and readily available means of adding flavour to many dishes. Which type of cider you use for different recipes is a matter of personal preference, and worth a little experimenting. Of the bottled ciders, vintage or still, dry cider is perhaps the most generally useful, especially for fish or beef dishes. A medium cider is good with fatty meats such as pork, ham, sausages and lamb; a medium to sweet cider for sweets and drinks.

Keeping wines and spirits

Table wines

The great enemies of wine are air and warmth. Keep unopened bottles lying horizontally (so that the cork remains moist) in a cool place. A wine rack is not essential, bottles will stack neatly on top of one another provided you arrange 'stoppers' to prevent the end bottles rolling away. Once opened a bottle of wine should be used up within a few days, keeping it cool and tightly corked meanwhile. (Spare plastic bottle caps come in useful here.) Small amounts are best transferred to small bottles to reduce the air space. The storage life of a white wine can be extended a little by keeping it in a refrigerator. Red wines keep longer if you can add drainings of sherry, port or brandy.

Fortified wines and vermouths

Store unopened bottles in a cool place. For cooking purposes, opened bottles will keep for a month or two, but they do not keep in good condition indefinitely, especially light sherries or vermouths.

Spirits and liqueurs

Store upright in a cool place. Spirits and liqueurs do not deteriorate for a long time after the bottles are opened. Do not expose to the air more than necessary, keep stoppered to prevent evaporation.

Oven temperatures

Description	Electric setting	Gas Mark
very cool	225°F – 110°C	¼
	250°F – 130°C	½
cool	275°F – 140°C	1
	300°F – 150°C	2
very moderate	325°F – 170°C	3
moderate	350°F – 180°C	4
moderate to	375°F – 190°C	5
moderately hot	400°F – 200°C	6
hot	425°F – 220°C	7
	450°F – 230°C	8
	475°F – 240°C	9

A note on metrication

In this book a basic equivalent of 25 grammes to 1 ounce has been used for solid measures and decilitres (tenths of a litre) used for liquid measures.

The exceptions to this rule are the more critical recipes, e.g., cake recipes, where more exact measures are needed.

All about flaming

Unless you have the confidence born of frequent practice or the aplomb of a head waiter it may be better to confine the flaming of a dish to the kitchen. This way you can make a confident entrance bearing the dramatically flaming dish, your guests are spared any possible smell of methylated spirits and you the expense of special equipment.

The whole purpose of flaming is to enhance and refine the flavour of a dish. What happens is that the alcohol and all excess fat are consumed in the flames, leaving behind the concentrated flavouring essences of the spirit or liqueur used.

It follows from this that the best wines and spirits for flaming are those which combine concentrated flavour with a high proof spirit. Brandy and rum meet both requirements and are particularly effective. The residual flavour of brandy is good with shellfish and meat dishes while rum has a particular affinity with certain fruits. Your Christmas pudding will be happy with either. Whisky, too, is sometimes used for flaming, and in Normandy they use their native apple brandy, Calvados. Many liqueurs are excellent for flaming puddings, especially those orange-flavoured varieties which have a high proof spirit. In spite of their relatively low proof spirit, heated table wines will also burn, but there is little residual flavour and therefore no point unless to remove the harshness of a very coarse wine.

Tricks of the trade

If a dish fails to flame it is usually because the spirit is cold. Release the alcohol by warming the spirit in a soup ladle or tiny saucepan and it will catch fire readily. The safest way to ignite it is at arm's length via a lighted taper. If you use a match avert your face just in case the flames leap high – as they can do if the dish contains much excess fat, which will add to the flame.

A waiter's trick to ensure a better and longer lasting blaze is to sprinkle sugar over the dish before flaming it. But go easily because this really works, and the residual caramel all adds to the flavour of such dishes as Bananas flamed with rum, Crêpes suzette or the Christmas pudding.

Once the dish is ablaze, shake the pan gently to distribute flames and spoon liquid over the food. If you can delay serving the dish for 2 to 3 minutes after flaming, the sauce will be even more mellow.

It is a mistake to think that food is flamed only at the end of the cooking process. In many of the great classic French recipes the meat or shellfish is flamed at an early stage, partly to remove excess grease and partly to refine and mellow the sauce by longer cooking with the spirit essences. When time and expense allow this really does pay dividends in the form of enhanced flavour.

Some famous flambé recipes follow.

Gaelic steak flambé

Cooking time: 9–10 minutes
Serves: 4

IMPERIAL	METRIC	AMERICAN
2 oz. butter	50 g. butter	¼ cup butter
2 tablespoons oil	2 tablespoons oil	3 tablespoons oil
1 medium onion, finely chopped	1 medium onion, finely chopped	1 medium onion, finely chopped
4 sirloin steaks, about ½ inch thick	4 sirloin steaks, about 1 cm. thick	4 sirloin steaks, about ½ inch thick
freshly ground black pepper	freshly ground black pepper	freshly ground black pepper
2 tablespoons chopped parsley	2 tablespoons chopped parsley	3 tablespoons chopped parsley
salt	salt	salt
2 tablespoons Irish whiskey	2 tablespoons Irish whiskey	3 tablespoons Irish whiskey

Melt the butter in a large frying pan with the oil. Add the onion and fry gently for about 5 minutes, until the onion just begins to colour. Rub the steaks well with freshly ground black pepper and place in the pan. Fry quickly for about 2 minutes on each side (longer if you like your steak well done). Add the parsley and some salt.

Pour the whiskey into a heated spoon, set alight and pour over the steaks. After the flames die down, turn the steaks and cook for another 30 seconds. Serve the steaks with the pan juices poured over.

Flamed veal kidneys

Cooking time: about 15 minutes
Serves: 4

IMPERIAL	METRIC	AMERICAN
3 veal kidneys, about 1¼ lb.	3 veal kidneys, about 600 g.	3 veal kidneys, about 1¼ lb.
1 oz. butter	25 g. butter	2 tablespoons butter
1 tablespoon vegetable oil	1 tablespoon vegetable oil	1 tablespoon vegetable oil
1 tablespoon chopped onion *or* shallot	1 tablespoon chopped onion *or* shallot	1 tablespoon chopped onion *or* shallot
4 oz. sliced button mushrooms	100 g. sliced button mushrooms	1 cup sliced button mushrooms
¼ pint thickened brown sauce *or* gravy	1½ dl. thickened brown sauce *or* gravy	⅔ cup thickened brown sauce *or* gravy
3 tablespoons Madeira *or* medium dry sherry	3 tablespoons Madeira *or* medium dry sherry	¼ cup Madeira *or* medium dry sherry
⅓ pint double cream	2 dl. double cream	generous ¾ cup whipping cream
3 tablespoons brandy	3 tablespoons brandy	¼ cup brandy
1 teaspoon French mustard	1 teaspoon French mustard	1 teaspoon prepared French mustard
salt and pepper	salt and pepper	salt and pepper

The trick with kidneys is to avoid overcooking or rapid boiling which will toughen and spoil them. Remove any fat or skin from the kidneys and cut across into ¼-inch slices. Melt the butter and oil in a frying pan and when hot fry the kidneys *briskly* for 3 to 4 minutes, turning to cook evenly. Remove to a chafing dish or flameproof serving dish, cover and keep warm. In the same fat, fry the onion very gently for several minutes then add the mushrooms and fry for another minute. Stir in the brown sauce and the wine, and bubble for several minutes until reduced and thickened. Add the cream and continue simmering until sauce is a thick coating consistency. (Unless thick it will be too thin after adding to the kidneys and their juices.) Meanwhile, pour the brandy into a heated ladle, ignite, and pour over the warm kidneys, shaking the pan gently until the flames die. Pour the sauce over the kidneys and mix gently, adding the mustard and seasoning to taste. Reheat carefully without boiling.

Bombe Vesuvius

Cooking time: 2–3 minutes
Temperature: 450°F., 230°C., Gas Mark 8
Serves: 6

IMPERIAL	METRIC	AMERICAN
1 baked sponge round	1 baked sponge round	1 baked sponge round
5–6 tablespoons Grand Marnier	5–6 tablespoons Grand Marnier	⅓–½ cup Grand Marnier
4 egg whites	4 egg whites	4 egg whites
6 oz. castor sugar	175 g. castor sugar	¾ cup granulated sugar
1 pint bought vanilla bombe, hard frozen*	½–¾ litre bought vanilla bombe, hard frozen*	3 cups bought vanilla bombe, hard frozen*

Preheat the very hot oven. Set the sponge on a flat ovenproof dish. Sprinkle with half the liqueur. Whisk the egg whites until very stiff and dry, add half the sugar and whisk until again stiff, then gently fold in the remaining sugar.

Place the ice cream bombe on the sponge and cover *completely* with meringue, drawing it up to a thick summit on top of the bombe. Sink a half egg shell into the summit so that it is concealed by the meringue. Sprinkle the whole with castor sugar and put into the preheated oven until the meringue is crisp and tinged with gold, about 2 to 3 minutes. Immediately fill the egg shell with heated liqueur (or brandy), ignite and serve flaming.

*Or make your own using recipe for Glace Bénédictine (see page 70) but omit the liqueur, and freeze hard in a pint size pudding basin.

Bananas flamed with rum

Cooking time: about 30 minutes
Temperature: 375°F., 190°C., Gas Mark 5
Serves: 4

IMPERIAL	METRIC	AMERICAN
4 firm bananas	4 firm bananas	4 firm bananas
a little flour	a little flour	a little flour
2 oz. butter	50 g. butter	$\frac{1}{4}$ cup butter
2 tablespoons castor sugar	2 tablespoons castor sugar	3 tablespoons granulated sugar
2–3 tablespoons rum	2–3 tablespoons rum	3–4 tablespoons rum
fresh cream	fresh cream	fresh cream

Peel the bananas and coat with flour. Melt the butter in a pan and over low heat fry the bananas until golden, turning once. Arrange side by side in a flameproof dish, dust thickly with sugar and cook near the top of the preheated oven, until the sugar starts to caramelise, about 20 minutes.

When ready to serve, pour the rum into a heated ladle, ignite and pour flaming over the bananas. Shake the pan gently to distribute the flames and serve the bananas on hot plates as soon as the flames die down. Pass the cream separately.

Note. If to be flamed at table, add the sugar to the chafing dish and cook slowly until the bananas are soft and the sugar has melted. Flame as before.

Crêpes suzette

(illustrated on back cover)
Cooking time: about 30 minutes plus 10 minutes later
Temperature: 425°F., 220°C., Gas Mark 7
Serves: 4

IMPERIAL	METRIC	AMERICAN
4 oz. plain flour	100 g. plain flour	1 cup all-purpose flour
1 tablespoon castor sugar	1 tablespoon castor sugar	1 tablespoon granulated sugar
1 egg and 1 yolk	1 egg and 1 yolk	1 egg and 1 yolk
$\frac{1}{2}$ pint milk and water mixed	3 dl. milk and water mixed	$1\frac{1}{4}$ cups milk and water mixed
1 tablespoon melted butter *or* oil	1 tablespoon melted butter *or* oil	1 tablespoon melted butter *or* oil
1 tablespoon brandy	1 tablespoon brandy	1 tablespoon brandy
suzette butter	*suzette butter*	*suzette butter*
3 oz. unsalted butter	75 g. unsalted butter	6 tablespoons sweet butter
3 oz. castor sugar	75 g. castor sugar	6 tablespoons granulated sugar
finely grated rind 1 large orange	finely grated rind 1 large orange	finely grated rind 1 large orange
2 tablespoons Grand Marnier *or* Cointreau	2 tablespoons Grand Marnier *or* Cointreau	3 tablespoons Grand Marnier *or* Cointreau
to flame	*to flame*	*to flame*
2–3 tablespoons brandy *or* liqueur	2–3 tablespoons brandy *or* liqueur	3–4 tablespoons brandy *or* liqueur

A famous flamed dish for which restaurants charge the earth. But in fact the eating quality is much better if the pancakes are filled with suzette butter and reheated *in the oven* so that they retain a degree of crispness instead of becoming flannelly.

Make the batter by sifting the flour and sugar into a mixing bowl, dropping the eggs into a 'well' formed in the centre and mixing to a smooth batter with the milk and water. (If you have an electric blender put the liquid in first and the flour last, and blend at top speed for 1 minute.) Leave to stand for 1 to 2 hours and just before using stir in the butter or oil and the spirit. Cook *wafer thin* pancakes in a small frying pan filmed with butter. This quantity will make 10 to 12 pancakes in a 6- to 7-inch pan. Stack one on top of the other and leave covered until needed.

Make suzette butter by creaming together the butter, sugar and rind then working in the liqueur. Spread each pancake generously with this butter and roll up. Arrange side by side in a flameproof dish. All this can be done in advance. Shortly before serving sprinkle with sugar and heat through in a hot oven for 5 to 8 minutes. Immediately before serving pour brandy into a heated ladle, ignite and pour flaming over the pancakes. The server should tilt the dish and spoon the flaming liqueur over the pancakes until the blaze dies down.

Apples flamed with rum

(illustrated on page 59)
Cooking time: 30 minutes
Serves: 4

IMPERIAL	METRIC	AMERICAN
1 pint water	generous ½ litre water	2½ cups water
4 oz. brown sugar	100 g. brown sugar	½ cup brown sugar, firmly packed
1 tablespoon lemon juice	1 tablespoon lemon juice	1 tablespoon lemon juice
1 teaspoon ground cinnamon	1 teaspoon ground cinnamon	1 teaspoon ground cinnamon
8 medium dessert apples	8 medium dessert apples	8 medium dessert apples
2 tablespoons sieved apricot jam	2 tablespoons sieved apricot jam	3 tablespoons sieved apricot jam
1 oz. butter	25 g. butter	2 tablespoons butter
castor sugar	castor sugar	granulated sugar
5–6 tablespoons rum	5–6 tablespoons rum	⅓–½ cup rum
thick fresh cream	thick fresh cream	thick fresh cream

In a wide saucepan heat the water, sugar, lemon juice and cinnamon until the sugar dissolves. Boil gently for several minutes. Peel the apples and drop immediately into the hot syrup, turning to coat all over. Poach very, very gently until the apples are *just* tender but not mushy, turning once. Drain, arrange in a flameproof dish and keep warm in a low oven.

Meanwhile, boil the syrup furiously until reduced to about ¼ pint (1½ dl.). Stir in the apricot jam and butter and, when hot, pour over the apples. Sprinkle lightly with sugar. Heat the rum, ignite and pour flaming over the apples. Serve immediately with thick fresh cream handed separately.

Peach floretta

Cooking time: 2 hours
Serves: 4

IMPERIAL	METRIC	AMERICAN
2 oz. round grain rice	50 g. round grain rice	¼ cup short grain rice
1½ oz. castor sugar	40 g. castor sugar	3 tablespoons granulated sugar
¾ pint milk	scant ½ litre milk	2 cups milk
1 tablespoon marmalade	1 tablespoon marmalade	1 tablespoon marmalade
¼ pint double cream	1½ dl. double cream	⅔ cup whipping cream
2–3 tablespoons Cointreau	2–3 tablespoons Cointreau	3–4 tablespoons Cointreau
4–6 canned peach halves	4–6 canned peach halves	4–6 canned peach halves
4–6 sugar cubes	4–6 sugar cubes	4–6 sugar cubes

Put the rice, castor sugar and milk in the top half of a double boiler. Cook over gently boiling water, stirring now and then, until the rice is soft and the milk absorbed, about 2 hours. Remove from the heat and stir in the marmalade. Leave to cool. When cold, fold in the lightly whipped cream and liqueur to taste.

Turn into a shallow dish. Lightly press the well drained peach halves, hollow-side up, into the rice.

Immediately before serving, soak the sugar cubes in *heated* liqueur, place one in each peach and light with a taper. The effect is charming, especially in a darkened room.

Meal starters

There is practically no limit to the variety of foods you can serve to start a meal. Being the 'curtain-raiser', so to speak, it should be something very good of its kind, stimulating to the taste buds and appealing to the eye. Naturally you will first consider the time of year – what's in season and consequently at its cheapest and best. And secondly, the weather – thick soups and substantial pâtés only in cold weather, when the rest of the meal is on the light side or your guests are known to be ravenous. For many, smoked fish are among the most attractive meal starters, while for others the tang of fresh fruit or the crispness of salad are unfailing appetite ticklers.

This chapter offers a mixed bag of ideas in which a little wine makes all the difference or provides the surprise element in otherwise everyday foods. The recipes range from the slight to the substantial, and for those to whom time matters they can all be partly if not wholly prepared in advance.

Highland prawn cocottes

Cooking time: 10 minutes
Serves: 4

IMPERIAL	METRIC	AMERICAN
1 oz. butter	25 g. butter	2 tablespoons butter
1 tablespoon finely chopped onion	1 tablespoon finely chopped onion	1 tablespoon finely chopped onion
8 oz. shelled prawns *or* shrimps	225 g. shelled prawns *or* shrimps	1½ cups shelled prawns *or* shrimp
2 tablespoons double cream	2 tablespoons double cream	3 tablespoons whipping cream
1 tablespoon Scotch whisky	1 tablespoon Scotch whisky	1 tablespoon Scotch whisky
2 tablespoons grated Cheddar cheese	2 tablespoons grated Cheddar cheese	3 tablespoons grated Cheddar cheese

Heat the butter in a saucepan and fry the onion very gently until soft and golden. Stir in the prawns or shrimps, then add the cream and stir over low heat until thoroughly hot. Stir in the whisky. Put into individual flameproof cocottes, sprinkle with cheese and brown lightly under the grill. Serve hot.

Grape and grapefruit cocktail

Serves: 4

IMPERIAL	METRIC	AMERICAN
3 medium grapefruit	3 medium grapefruit	3 medium grapefruit
3 oz. sweet black *or* white grapes	75 g. sweet black *or* white grapes	¾ cup sweet purple *or* green grapes
3 tablespoons castor sugar	3 tablespoons castor sugar	¼ cup granulated sugar
2–3 tablespoons brandy	2–3 tablespoons brandy	3–4 tablespoons brandy
grapes and mint sprigs	grapes and mint sprigs	grapes and mint sprigs

With a sharp knife peel the grapefruit, cutting off the inner white skin as well as the outer peel. Cut out each segment, free of skin and membrane, and put into a basin. Squeeze juice from empty membranes over segments. Halve and de-seed grapes and add to grapefruit with the sugar and brandy. Stir and cover.

Leave to marinate for an hour, preferably in the refrigerator. Serve in individual glasses garnished with grapes and mint.

Mushrooms stewed in oil and wine

Cooking time: 10–12 minutes
Serves: 4

IMPERIAL	METRIC	AMERICAN
¼ pint olive oil	1½ dl. olive oil	⅔ cup olive oil
¼ pint water	1½ dl. water	⅔ cup water
4 tablespoons white wine	4 tablespoons white wine	⅓ cup white wine
2 tablespoons lemon juice	2 tablespoons lemon juice	3 tablespoons lemon juice
2 tablespoons chopped onion	2 tablespoons chopped onion	3 tablespoons chopped onion
1 teaspoon tomato purée	1 teaspoon tomato purée	1 teaspoon tomato paste
1 bay leaf	1 bay leaf	1 bay leaf
salt and ground black pepper	salt and ground black pepper	salt and ground black pepper
1 lb. small button mushrooms	450 g. small button mushrooms	1 lb. small button mushrooms

Put all ingredients except mushrooms into a pan and allow to simmer for 5 minutes. Wash the mushrooms and add to the pan. Simmer for 5 to 8 minutes, stirring occasionally. Drain mushrooms and arrange in individual shallow dishes.

Reduce liquid to a syrupy consistency by boiling rapidly for a minute or two, then pour over the mushrooms. These succulent mushrooms make a delicious meal starter, or they can be served as part of a mixed hors d'oeuvre.

Leeks in red wine

Cooking time: 15–20 minutes
Serves: 4

IMPERIAL	METRIC	AMERICAN
8 medium leeks	8 medium leeks	8 medium leeks
4 tablespoons olive oil	4 tablespoons olive oil	⅓ cup olive oil
¼ pint robust red wine	1½ dl. robust red wine	⅔ cup robust red wine
4 tablespoons stock *or* water	4 tablespoons stock *or* water	⅓ cup stock *or* water
salt and pepper	salt and pepper	salt and pepper

Trim leeks almost down to the white part and clean very thoroughly in salted water. Drain well. Heat the oil in a large pan and fry the leeks slowly, turning, until golden brown. Pour in the wine; let it bubble for a minute or so, then add stock or water and check seasoning. Cover, and cook, turning once, for about 10 minutes until tender.

Put the leeks into a shallow dish, then reduce the wine and stock a little by rapid boiling before pouring over the leeks. May be served hot or cold.

Button onions with raisins

Cooking time: 1¼ hours
Serves: 4

IMPERIAL	METRIC	AMERICAN
1½ oz. butter	40 g. butter	3 tablespoons butter
1 tablespoon olive oil	1 tablespoon olive oil	1 tablespoon olive oil
1 lb. button onions, peeled	450 g. button onions, peeled	1 lb. tiny onions, peeled
3 oz. seedless raisins *or* sultanas	75 g. seedless raisins *or* sultanas	⅔ cup seedless dark *or* white raisins
sprig each thyme and parsley	sprig each thyme and parsley	sprig each thyme and parsley
1 small bay leaf	1 small bay leaf	1 small bay leaf
salt and pepper	salt and pepper	salt and pepper
½ pint white wine	3 dl. white wine	1¼ cups white wine

Melt the butter and oil in a flameproof casserole or strong saucepan. Add the onions and cook over low heat, shaking frequently until golden, about 10 minutes. Drain off the fat. Add the raisins, herbs, seasonings and wine. Cover closely and simmer *very gently* for 1 hour.

Using a perforated spoon, transfer the onions and raisins to a shallow serving dish (or individual dishes) and discard the herbs. Reduce the wine to a syrupy consistency by rapid boiling, then pour over the onions. Serve cold, alone, as part of a mixed hors d'oeuvre, or with a pâté.

Quick chicken liver pâté

(illustrated on page 19)
Cooking time: about 7 minutes
Serves: 4

IMPERIAL	METRIC	AMERICAN
8 oz. chicken livers	225 g. chicken livers	$\frac{1}{2}$ lb. chicken livers
2½ oz. butter	65 g. butter	5 tablespoons butter
1 cut garlic clove	1 cut garlic clove	1 cut garlic clove
1½ tablespoons sherry *or* Madeira	1½ tablespoons sherry *or* Madeira	2 tablespoons sherry *or* Madeira
1½ tablespoons brandy	1½ tablespoons brandy	2 tablespoons brandy
salt and black pepper	salt and black pepper	salt and black pepper
pinch mixed spice	pinch mixed spice	pinch mixed spice

Rinse the livers in cold water and remove any membranes or discoloured pieces. Melt 1 oz. of the butter in a small saucepan over low heat and sauté the livers, until firm but still pink inside, about 3 to 4 minutes. When cooked, drain and transfer them to a basin previously rubbed with the garlic. Add the sherry and brandy to the juices remaining in the pan, bring to the boil and remove from the heat.

Mash and pound the livers to a paste, add to them generous seasonings of salt and pepper, the spice, the remaining butter (softened if necessary) and the liquid from the pan. Mix very thoroughly, then pack into small pots or a dish. Cover and leave to become cold. Garnish with parsley and serve with hot toast.

Chicken-stuffed mushrooms

Cooking time: 20 minutes
Temperature: 350°F., 180°C., Gas Mark 4
Serves: 4

IMPERIAL	METRIC	AMERICAN
8 large flat mushrooms	8 large flat mushrooms	8 large flat mushrooms
3 oz. butter	75 g. butter	6 tablespoons butter
2 tablespoons chopped green pepper *or* onion	2 tablespoons chopped green pepper *or* onion	3 tablespoons chopped green sweet pepper *or* onion
6 oz. cooked chicken, finely chopped	175 g. cooked chicken, finely chopped	1 cup finely chopped cooked chicken
1 tablespoon medium dry sherry	1 tablespoon medium dry sherry	1 tablespoon medium dry sherry
1–2 tablespoons chicken stock *or* soup	1–2 tablespoons chicken stock *or* soup	1–3 tablespoons chicken stock *or* soup
2 oz. grated Parmesan *or* dry Cheddar	50 g. grated Parmesan *or* dry Cheddar	$\frac{1}{2}$ cup grated Parmesan *or* dry Cheddar

Wipe the mushrooms and remove the stalks. Chop the stalks finely. Melt butter in a saucepan and turn the mushroom caps in it before arranging them in a single layer in a shallow ovenproof dish.

In remaining butter, gently fry the chopped pepper (or onion) and mushroom stalks until soft. Stir in the chicken, sherry and sufficient stock to bind mixture together. Divide between mushroom caps, making a neat pile on each. Sprinkle with cheese. Cover dish, and heat through in the preheated oven.

Roquefort celery bites

Serves: 4

IMPERIAL	METRIC	AMERICAN
3 oz. stale Roquefort cheese	75 g. stale Roquefort cheese	3 oz. stale Roquefort cheese
1 oz. softened butter	25 g. softened butter	2 tablespoons softened butter
1 tablespoon single cream	1 tablespoon single cream	1 tablespoon coffee cream
1 tablespoon brandy	1 tablespoon brandy	1 tablespoon brandy
3–4 small sticks crisp celery	3–4 small sticks crisp celery	3–4 small stalks crisp celery

Press the cheese through a strainer then blend with butter and cream, beating until fluffy. Flavour to taste with brandy. Put into a piping bag fitted with a star nozzle and pipe the mixture neatly along the length of the celery sticks. With a sharp knife cut into bite-size pieces.

Mystery cheese canapés

Makes: 24

IMPERIAL	METRIC	AMERICAN
basic mixture	*basic mixture*	*basic mixture*
6 oz. finely grated mild Cheddar cheese	175 g. finely grated mild Cheddar cheese	1½ cups finely grated mild Cheddar cheese
1 oz. softened butter	25 g. softened butter	2 tablespoons softened butter
3 tablespoons single cream	3 tablespoons single cream	¼ cup coffee cream
shake of cayenne *or* curry powder	shake of cayenne *or* curry powder	shake of cayenne *or* curry powder
Drambuie, Chartreuse and medium dry sherry	Drambuie, Chartreuse and medium dry sherry	Drambuie, Chartreuse and medium dry sherry
bite-size crisp cocktail biscuits	bite-size crisp cocktail biscuits	bite-size crisp cocktail crackers
paprika	paprika	paprika
salted almonds	salted almonds	salted almonds
chopped parsley	chopped parsley	chopped parsley

Play a guessing game with your guests by offering with before-meal drinks an assortment of wine-flavoured canapés. Prepare basic mixture by blending cheese, butter and cream together until fluffy. Season lightly with a whisper of cayenne or curry powder.

Divide the mixture into three and flavour each portion to taste with either Drambuie, Chartreuse or sherry, starting with no more than a teaspoon of each. Don't overdo it. Pile a small teaspoonful of mixture on each cocktail biscuit, topping the Drambuie ones with a shake of paprika, sherry ones with a salted almond and Chartreuse ones with a flick of chopped parsley.

Marinated kipper fillets

Serves: 4

IMPERIAL	METRIC	AMERICAN
4 boned and filleted kippers *or* 2 packets kipper fillets	4 boned and filleted kippers *or* 2 packets kipper fillets	4 boned and filleted kippers *or* 2 packages kipper fillets
4 tablespoons medium dry white wine	4 tablespoons medium dry white wine	⅓ cup medium dry white wine
4 tablespoons olive oil	4 tablespoons olive oil	⅓ cup olive oil
2 tablespoons lemon juice	2 tablespoons lemon juice	3 tablespoons lemon juice
few onion rings	few onion rings	few onion rings
8 peppercorns	8 peppercorns	8 peppercorns
4 bay leaves	4 bay leaves	4 bay leaves
lemon wedges	lemon wedges	lemon wedges

Put the kipper fillets in a dish with the wine, oil, lemon juice, onion rings, peppercorns and bay leaves. Leave in a cool place for 24 hours. No cooking is needed. Drain and garnish with lemon wedges. Serve with thin slices of bread and butter formed into rolls.

Open sandwiches using marinated kipper fillets
Use these, combined with: scrambled eggs on pumpernickel; lettuce and cucumber on white bread; hard-boiled eggs on brown bread; tomato and onion rings on white bread; cottage cheese on crispbread with stuffed olives.

Melon cocktail

Serves: 4

IMPERIAL	METRIC	AMERICAN
1 large ripe melon	1 large ripe melon	1 large ripe melon
castor sugar	castor sugar	granulated sugar
Cointreau	Cointreau	Cointreau
4 thin slices lemon	4 thin slices lemon	4 thin slices lemon
4 glacé cherries	4 glacé cherries	4 candied cherries

Cut melon into four and remove seeds and rind. Cut the flesh into small cubes. Put into a basin with sugar to taste. Sprinkle with Cointreau (allowing one tablespoonful to 6 tablespoonfuls melon). Mix well, cover tightly, and chill for at least an hour in the refrigerator. Serve in glasses and decorate with a slice of lemon and a cherry.

Variation *Manhattan melon cocktail*
Omit the Cointreau and sprinkle the melon sparingly with Anisette. For Anisette lovers only.

Sunny island salad

Serves: 4

IMPERIAL	METRIC	AMERICAN
4 large firm ripe tomatoes	4 large firm ripe tomatoes	4 large firm ripe tomatoes
½ green honeydew melon	½ green honeydew melon	½ green honeydew melon
2 bananas	2 bananas	2 bananas
2 tablespoons lemon juice	2 tablespoons lemon juice	3 tablespoons lemon juice
salt and pepper	salt and pepper	salt and pepper
1 recipe Paradise dressing (page 24)	1 recipe Paradise dressing (page 24)	1 recipe Paradise dressing (page 24)

Peel the tomatoes and cut them into quarters. Remove seeds and juice and reserve for a soup or stew. Cut the melon into six pieces; cut the flesh into chunks (keep the skin for garnishing). Peel the bananas, cut into slices and turn them in the lemon juice. Mix melon and banana, season lightly and pile mixture on a flat dish.

Cut melon skins in half and arrange alternately round the edge of the dish with some of the tomato quarters. Slice remaining tomatoes and scatter the shreds over the salad. Serve Paradise dressing (which can be made well in advance) separately.

Prawn and tomato medley

Cooking time: 7–10 minutes
Serves: 4

IMPERIAL	METRIC	AMERICAN
¼ pint fresh unpeeled prawns	1½ dl. fresh unpeeled prawns	⅔ cup fresh unshelled prawns *or* shrimp
6 oz. canned *or* frozen peeled prawns	175 g. canned *or* frozen peeled prawns	1 cup canned *or* frozen shelled prawns *or* shrimp
1 small egg, well beaten	1 small egg, well beaten	1 egg, well beaten
2 oz. fresh white breadcrumbs	50 g. fresh white breadcrumbs	1 cup fresh white bread crumbs
12 oz. ripe firm tomatoes	350 g. ripe firm tomatoes	4 ripe firm medium tomatoes
2 oz. butter	50 g. butter	¼ cup butter
2 oz. finely chopped mushrooms	50 g. finely chopped mushrooms	½ cup finely chopped mushrooms
2 oz. finely chopped ham	50 g. finely chopped ham	⅓ cup finely chopped ham
2 tablespoons medium dry sherry	2 tablespoons medium dry sherry	3 tablespoons medium dry sherry
salt, pepper and paprika	salt, pepper and paprika	salt, pepper and paprika

Peel all but three of the fresh prawns. Drain and dry the canned or frozen prawns. Turn all the peeled prawns in the beaten egg, then toss in the breadcrumbs. Peel and quarter the tomatoes, remove the seeds and juice (these can be added to soups or stews) and cut the flesh into neat shreds.

Melt the butter in a frying pan and gently cook the mushrooms for a few minutes. Add the ham, coated prawns, and shredded tomato. Cook gently together, turning carefully, until thoroughly hot. Stir in the sherry and seasoning to taste. Garnish with the reserved whole prawns. If you have a suitable pan this dish can be served in the pan in which it was cooked.

Soups

This is not a subject to merit a long chapter but there are some soups which can be lifted from the everyday into the gourmet class with the aid of a dash of wine. But 'dash' is the operative word, as too much wine can ruin the flavour.

Table wines can be used to strengthen and enrich the flavour of certain home-made soups when they are added at the *beginning* and cooked with the soup; white wines in fish or poultry soups, robust red wines in kidney/game soups.

Perhaps the most effective are fortified wines added to meat, poultry or game soups *immediately* before serving. Use a medium dry sherry or port, or a dry Madeira, starting with not more than one tablespoon per pint, tasting as you go, and remembering the aim is to enhance the natural flavour of the soup – not to overwhelm it. When time does not permit the luxury of a home-made soup try experimenting with canned and packet soups. With either kind, put a little of the same hot soup in several cups and add a few drops of various wines to each; then taste and compare . . . and you will soon know what you like. Some generally acceptable additions are Madeira or sherry with consommé or clear turtle; brandy or sherry with shellfish bisques; port or sherry with tomato or game; sherry with chicken or mushroom.

French onion soup

Cooking time: about 45 minutes
Serves: 4

IMPERIAL	METRIC	AMERICAN
1½ oz. butter	40 g. butter	3 tablespoons butter
1 tablespoon oil	1 tablespoon oil	1 tablespoon oil
1 lb. Spanish onions, thinly sliced	450 g. Spanish onions, thinly sliced	4 medium Spanish onions, thinly sliced
2 teaspoons brown sugar	2 teaspoons brown sugar	2 teaspoons brown sugar
1¾ pints boiling beef stock *or* water plus stock cube	1 litre boiling beef stock *or* water plus stock cube	4¼ cups boiling beef stock *or* water plus bouillon cube
4 tablespoons dry white wine	4 tablespoons dry white wine	⅓ cup dry white wine
salt and pepper	salt and pepper	salt and pepper
4 slices French bread	4 slices French bread	4 slices French bread
grated Gruyère *or* Parmesan cheese	grated Gruyère *or* Parmesan cheese	grated Gruyère *or* Parmesan cheese

Heat the butter and oil in a heavy pan, add onions and stir. Cover and cook over *low* heat until soft, 10 to 12 minutes. Stir in the sugar, cover and continue cooking over moderate heat until onions are a deep golden brown. Add the stock, wine and seasonings to taste. Cover, and simmer gently for at least 30 minutes. Meanwhile, toast the bread slowly. To serve, put a bread croûte into each earthenware bowl and pour boiling soup over. Hand the cheese separately.

Note. This is a wonderful cold weather soup. The longer you cook it the deeper and richer the flavour, and it is even better reheated next day. And if you feel inclined you can greatly increase its 'warming' power by adding 2 tablespoons of brandy.

Kidney soup

Cooking time: about 2¼ hours
Serves: 4

IMPERIAL	METRIC	AMERICAN
8 oz. ox kidney	225 g. ox kidney	½ lb. beef kidney
1 oz. dripping	25 g. dripping	2 tablespoons drippings
1 onion, sliced	1 onion, sliced	1 onion, sliced
1½ tablespoons flour	1½ tablespoons flour	2 tablespoons flour
1¼ pints meat stock	¾ litre meat stock	3 cups meat stock
¼ pint robust red wine	1½ dl. robust red wine	⅔ cup robust red wine
1 carrot, sliced	1 carrot, sliced	1 carrot, sliced
1 stick celery, sliced	1 stick celery, sliced	1 stalk celery, sliced
1 bay leaf	1 bay leaf	1 bay leaf
small piece mace	small piece mace	small piece mace
6 crushed peppercorns	6 crushed peppercorns	6 crushed peppercorns

Soak the kidney in cold salted water for 1 to 2 hours. Drain and slice. Melt the dripping and when hot fry the kidney briskly for a minute or so, then add the onion and fry gently for 5 minutes. Sprinkle in the flour, stir and cook slowly until flour is pale brown. Add the stock, wine, carrot, celery, bay leaf and spices.

Cover, simmer very gently for about 2 hours. Discard bay leaf, reserve a few pieces of kidney to chop for garnishing. Purée rest of the soup by passing through a mouli or electric blender. Reheat, check seasoning and add chopped kidney before serving.

Mussel soup

Cooking time: about 2¼ hours
Serves: 4

IMPERIAL	METRIC	AMERICAN
2½–3 pints small fresh mussels	1¼–1½ litres small fresh mussels	1½–2 quarts small fresh mussels
1 oz. butter	25 g. butter	2 tablespoons butter
1 clove garlic	1 clove garlic	1 clove garlic
1 stick celery, chopped	1 stick celery, chopped	1 stalk celery, chopped
3 oz. onion, chopped	75 g. onion, chopped	1 medium onion, chopped
8 oz. ripe tomatoes, skinned and chopped	225 g. ripe tomatoes, skinned and chopped	3 ripe tomatoes, skinned and chopped
6 tablespoons dry white wine	1¼ dl. dry white wine	½ cup dry white wine
6 tablespoons water	1¼ dl. water	½ cup water
ground black pepper	ground black pepper	ground black pepper
fresh chopped parsley	fresh chopped parsley	fresh chopped parsley

Scrub and scrape the mussels in several changes of cold water, discarding any that fail to shut tightly. Melt the butter in a wide pan and over low heat fry the garlic, celery and onion for 5 minutes or until soft and golden. Add the tomatoes and wine; allow to boil for 3 to 4 minutes then add the water. After another 2 minutes put in the mussels. Cover, and cook over quick heat, shaking the pan from time to time, until the mussels open, about 5 minutes. Throw away any mussels which fail to open.

Discard the shells as they open, and serve immediately with cooking liquor strained over. Season with a little ground black pepper and chopped parsley. Serve with crusty French bread and creamy butter.

Scallop bisque

Cooking time: 40–45 minutes
Serves: 4

IMPERIAL	METRIC	AMERICAN
2 tablespoons vegetable oil	2 tablespoons vegetable oil	3 tablespoons vegetable oil
1 carrot, sliced	1 carrot, sliced	1 carrot, sliced
1 leek, sliced	1 leek, sliced	1 leek, sliced
8 oz. white fish fillet, skinned	225 g. white fish fillet, skinned	½ lb. white fish fillet, skinned
2 tablespoons cornflour	2 tablespoons cornflour	3 tablespoons cornstarch
¼ pint white wine	1½ dl. white wine	⅔ cup white wine
¼ pint water	1½ dl. water	⅔ cup water
2 tablespoons tomato purée	2 tablespoons tomato purée	3 tablespoons tomato paste
1¼ pints milk	¾ litre milk	3 cups milk
4 scallops, cleaned	4 scallops, cleaned	4 scallops, cleaned
salt and pepper	salt and pepper	salt and pepper
3 tablespoons double cream	3 tablespoons double cream	¼ cup whipping cream

Heat the oil in a large pan and gently fry the carrot and leek for several minutes. Cut the white fish into cubes, add to the pan and stir and fry for another few minutes. Sprinkle in the cornflour and stir until fat is absorbed. Add the wine, water, tomato purée and stir until boiling. Add the milk.

Cover and cook very gently for 20 to 30 minutes. Pass through a sieve or liquidise in a blender, and return to the saucepan. All this can be done in advance.

Ten minutes or so before serving reheat soup, add scallops cut into small pieces and cook gently until tender. Adjust seasoning and stir in the cream.

Oxtail soup

Cooking time: about 4 hours
Serves: 5–6

IMPERIAL	METRIC	AMERICAN
1 small oxtail, jointed	1 small oxtail, jointed	1 small oxtail, jointed
1 oz. beef dripping	25 g. beef dripping	2 tablespoons beef drippings
1 onion	1 onion	1 onion
1 carrot	1 carrot	1 carrot
1 stick celery	1 stick celery	1 stalk celery
2½ pints water	1¼ litres water	6¼ cups water
salt	salt	salt
small bouquet of bay leaf, thyme and parsley	small bouquet of bay leaf, thyme and parsley	small bouquet of bay leaf, thyme and parsley
piece of mace	piece of mace	piece of mace
6 peppercorns	6 peppercorns	6 peppercorns
1 oz. flour	25 g. flour	¼ cup flour
3–4 tablespoons medium dry sherry	3–4 tablespoons medium dry sherry	¼–⅓ cup medium dry sherry

Remove any excess fat from tail. Heat dripping in a large frying pan and in it fry the pieces of meat until browned on all sides, then transfer to a large saucepan. Meanwhile, prepare and slice the vegetables and fry gently in the same dripping until golden then add to the meat. Cover the meat and vegetables with water, 1 teaspoon of salt, the herbs and spices and simmer very gently for 3 to 4 hours.

Strain the soup, return to the saucepan with some pieces of meat picked from the smaller bones. Blend the flour smoothly with the sherry, add to soup and stir until boiling. Check seasoning and simmer for several minutes before serving.

Note. The thicker pieces of meat can be served as stewed oxtail.

Thick cream of mushroom soup

Cooking time: about 10 minutes
Serves: 4–5

IMPERIAL	METRIC	AMERICAN
8 oz. mushrooms	225 g. mushrooms	½ lb. mushrooms
½ pint milk	3 dl. milk	1¼ cups milk
2 oz. butter	50 g. butter	¼ cup butter
1½ oz. plain flour	40 g. plain flour	6 tablespoons all-purpose flour
1 pint water	generous ½ litre water	2½ cups water
1 chicken stock cube	1 chicken stock cube	1 chicken bouillon cube
1–2 teaspoons lemon juice	1–2 teaspoons lemon juice	1–2 teaspoons lemon juice
salt and pepper if required	salt and pepper if required	salt and pepper if required
¼ pint single cream	1½ dl. single cream	⅔ cup coffee cream
2 tablespoons medium dry sherry	2 tablespoons medium dry sherry	3 tablespoons medium dry sherry
finely chopped parsley	finely chopped parsley	finely chopped parsley

Wipe the mushrooms, put into an electric blender with half the milk and reduce to a purée. Add the remaining milk. In a large saucepan melt the butter, add the flour and stir and cook over low heat for 2 minutes. Add the water and stock cube and bring to the boil, whisking briskly all the time. Add the mushroom and milk mixture and simmer for 5 minutes. Stir in the lemon juice and seasoning if required.

Shortly before serving add the cream, reheat, and flavour to taste with sherry. This is a rich soup so garnish very simply with a dusting of chopped parsley.

Quick chicken liver pâté (see recipe on page 13)

Cream of pheasant soup

Cooking time: about 3 hours
Serves: 4

IMPERIAL	METRIC	AMERICAN
carcases and pieces of 2 cooked pheasants	carcases and pieces of 2 cooked pheasants	carcases and pieces of 2 cooked pheasants
raw beef bone	raw beef bone	raw beef bone
1 onion stuck with a clove	1 onion stuck with a clove	1 onion stuck with a clove
1 stick celery, sliced	1 stick celery, sliced	1 stalk celery, sliced
2 carrots, sliced	2 carrots, sliced	2 carrots, sliced
bouquet of thyme, bay and parsley, tied	bouquet of thyme, bay and parsley, tied	bouquet of thyme, bay and parsley, tied
6 black peppercorns	6 black peppercorns	6 black peppercorns
salt	salt	salt
$2\frac{1}{2}$ pints water	$1\frac{1}{4}$ litres water	$6\frac{1}{4}$ cups water
2 tablespoons fresh breadcrumbs	2 tablespoons fresh breadcrumbs	3 tablespoons fresh bread crumbs
4 tablespoons sherry	4 tablespoons sherry	$\frac{1}{3}$ cup sherry
2 egg yolks	2 egg yolks	2 egg yolks
4 tablespoons double cream	4 tablespoons double cream	$\frac{1}{3}$ cup whipping cream

Break up the carcases and put with the pieces of pheasant and beef bone into a large pan. Add the vegetables, herbs, peppercorns, 1 teaspoon salt, and the water. Bring slowly to the boil, then cover and simmer very gently for $2\frac{1}{2}$ to 3 hours, until stock is well flavoured. Strain. Pick meat off the bones, put into electric blender with the breadcrumbs and a little of the stock. Return to the soup, reheat and add the sherry. Off the heat and, just before serving, stir in the egg yolks blended with the cream; do not boil after this. Check seasoning, and serve with croûtons of fried bread.

Cherry wine soup

Cooking time: about 10 minutes
Serves: 3–4

IMPERIAL	METRIC	AMERICAN
$\frac{1}{4}$ pint red wine	$1\frac{1}{2}$ dl. red wine	$\frac{2}{3}$ cup red wine
2 cloves	2 cloves	2 cloves
$\frac{1}{2}$-inch stick cinnamon	1-cm. stick cinnamon	$\frac{1}{2}$-inch stick cinnamon
thinly pared rind of half orange	thinly pared rind of half orange	thinly pared rind of half orange
1-lb. can stoned Morello cherries in syrup	450-g. can stoned Morello cherries in syrup	1-lb. can pitted Bing cherries in syrup
1 tablespoon sugar, or to taste	1 tablespoon sugar, or to taste	1 tablespoon sugar, or to taste
$\frac{3}{4}$ pint water	scant $\frac{1}{2}$ litre water	scant 2 cups water
$1\frac{1}{2}$ tablespoons cornflour	$1\frac{1}{2}$ tablespoons cornflour	2 tablespoons cornstarch
sour cream	sour cream	sour cream

Chilled fruit soups are popular in parts of Europe and make a refreshing change. Put the wine, cloves, cinnamon and orange rind into a small saucepan and simmer gently for 5 minutes. Strain the wine into a larger saucepan and add the cherries and their syrup, sugar and all but 3 tablespoons of the water. Bring slowly to boiling point.

Blend the cornflour smoothly with the remaining water, stir into the soup and stir until boiling. Simmer for 2 minutes, then turn into a basin and leave to cool, stirring occasionally. Serve chilled, with a spoonful of sour cream in the centre of each bowl.

Sauces and gravies

There is nothing very new about using wine in sauces. In seventeenth century England, when oysters were plentiful and cheap, the popular accompaniment with mutton was an oyster sauce containing white wine. And that delectable combination of orange juice, port and redcurrant jelly known as Cumberland sauce is still the ideal companion for ham or game. As you would expect, many French and Italian sauces contain wine, and recipes for a few of the simpler ones are included in this chapter.

There is no better use for half a glass of red or white table wine left in the bottom of a bottle than to pop it in a sauce or gravy. Even quite small amounts of wine will add body and flavour, but as always the wine must be cooked long enough to drive off the alcohol and the rawness.

Wine gravies

After dishing a roast joint or chicken and draining off the fat, pour half a cupful of any table wine into the roasting tin. Boil it hard for a minute or two, at the same time scraping up the coagulated essences from the bottom of the tin. Then add a little stock or water (and a gravy cube or powder if you prefer a thickened gravy) and simmer for a few minutes.

The same principle applies after frying or grilling liver, kidneys, chicken joints, chops or steaks. Stir the wine with the pan juices and boil briskly for a couple of minutes. If you like, stir in a few pieces of butter which will enrich and slightly thicken the sauce.

When grilling fish, add white wine to the grill pan and boil up as before. Makers of home-made apple wine say that it is excellent used this way.

Wine and cream sauces

White wine and cream make a perfect sauce for fried escalopes of veal, kidneys or chicken. When cooked, dish the meat, drain off excess fat and add, for 4 servings, $\frac{1}{4}$ pint of a medium dry white wine. Stir with pan juices then boil fast for 3 to 4 minutes or until reduced by half. Lower the heat and gradually stir in $\frac{1}{4}$ pint double cream. Stir and cook gently until the sauce thickens, which it will do in a few minutes, especially if the pan is a wide one. Add seasoning, and pour over the meat. When available you can add finely chopped fresh herbs (parsley, tarragon or chives), or a spoonful or two of Madeira.

Cumberland sauce

Cooking time: about 15 minutes
Serves: 6–8

IMPERIAL	METRIC	AMERICAN
2 large oranges	2 large oranges	2 large oranges
1 small lemon	1 small lemon	1 small lemon
8 oz. redcurrant jelly	225 g. redcurrant jelly	$\frac{2}{3}$ cup redcurrant jelly
1 tablespoon wine vinegar	1 tablespoon wine vinegar	1 tablespoon wine vinegar
2 teaspoons made mustard	2 teaspoons made mustard	2 teaspoons prepared mustard
6 tablespoons port	6 tablespoons port	$\frac{1}{2}$ cup port
1 tablespoon brown sugar	1 tablespoon brown sugar	1 tablespoon brown sugar
salt and pepper	salt and pepper	salt and pepper

Wash the oranges and lemon. Pare the rinds thinly with a potato peeler, cover with cold water and simmer for 10 minutes. Meanwhile, squeeze the orange and lemon juice and put into a saucepan with all the remaining ingredients. Heat gently, stirring, until all jelly dissolves, then simmer until ingredients are smoothly amalgamated.

Drain the rinds, cut into matchstick strips, add to the other ingredients and heat together for a few minutes. Serve cold.
Serve with: hot or cold ham, venison, turkey, pickled bacon or tongue.

Sauce espagnole

Cooking time: $\frac{1}{2}$–1 hour
Serves: 4

IMPERIAL	METRIC	AMERICAN
2 oz. pork *or* beef dripping	50 g. pork *or* beef dripping	$\frac{1}{4}$ cup pork *or* beef drippings
1 small onion, chopped	1 small onion, chopped	1 small onion, chopped
3 oz. lean bacon, chopped	75 g. lean bacon, chopped	$\frac{1}{2}$ cup chopped Canadian-style bacon
1 stick celery, chopped	1 stick celery, chopped	1 stalk celery, chopped
1 oz. flour	25 g. flour	$\frac{1}{4}$ cup flour
$\frac{3}{4}$ pint stock *or* water plus stock cube	scant $\frac{1}{2}$ litre stock *or* water plus stock cube	scant 2 cups stock *or* water plus bouillon cube
1 teaspoon tomato purée	1 teaspoon tomato purée	1 teaspoon tomato paste
sprig fresh *or* $\frac{1}{4}$ teaspoon dried parsley and thyme	sprig fresh *or* $\frac{1}{4}$ teaspoon dried parsley and thyme	sprig fresh *or* $\frac{1}{4}$ teaspoon dried parsley and thyme
1 small bay leaf	1 small bay leaf	1 small bay leaf
salt, sugar and pepper	salt, sugar and pepper	salt, sugar and pepper
1–2 tablespoons medium dry sherry	1–2 tablespoons medium dry sherry	1–3 tablespoons medium dry sherry

Heat the fat in a heavy saucepan and gently fry onion, bacon and celery for 5 minutes. Add the flour, and cook, stirring, allowing it *slowly* to turn nut brown. Add stock, tomato purée, herbs and seasonings, and whisk until boiling.

Cover and *simmer* gently for 30 to 60 minutes or longer (the longer you cook a brown sauce the finer the flavour), skimming off fat and scum now and then. Press through a strainer, reheat, add sherry and adjust seasoning. Final consistency should lightly coat back of a spoon, so if during cooking the sauce reduces too much, add a little more stock.

Variations

Sauce madère
Add 2 tablespoons Madeira half way through the cooking, and 2 tablespoons just before serving.
Use for: ham, beef fillet, veal and egg lishes.

Sauce périgueux
Add 4 tablespoons Madeira and the juice from a small can of truffles half way through the cooking. After straining the sauce, add 2 finely chopped truffles and 1 oz. butter.
Use for: beef fillet, ham, veal and egg dishes.

Sauce chasseur
Replace $\frac{1}{4}$ pint of the stock with dry white wine and add 2 large sliced tomatoes. After straining the sauce, add 4 oz. sliced mushrooms sautéed in 1 oz. butter and a tablespoon chopped fresh chervil, tarragon and parsley mixed.
Use for: chicken, veal, rabbit and egg dishes.

Sauce bigarade
Simmer the thinly pared rind of a Seville orange for 5 minutes in water, then cut into shreds. Add to the strained Sauce espagnole with the juice of the orange, a teaspoon of redcurrant jelly and one or more teaspoons of sugar. Simmer for 5 minutes.
Use for: duck, game or venison.

Cranberry and port wine sauce

Cooking time: about 10 minutes
Serves: 4

IMPERIAL	METRIC	AMERICAN
4 tablespoons water	4 tablespoons water	$\frac{1}{3}$ cup water
4 oz. granulated sugar	100 g. granulated sugar	$\frac{1}{2}$ cup granulated sugar
8 oz. cranberries	225 g. cranberries	2 cups cranberries
1 teaspoon grated orange rind	1 teaspoon grated orange rind	1 teaspoon grated orange rind
2–3 tablespoons port	2–3 tablespoons port	3–4 tablespoons port

Heat the water and sugar in a saucepan until the sugar dissolves. Add the washed cranberries and the orange rind and stew gently until the cranberries pop their skins and are quite tender, 5 to 8 minutes. Stir in the port and allow to cool.
Serve with: roast chicken or turkey.

Chicken Marengo (see recipe on page 37)

Sauce bercy

Cooking time: about 5 minutes
Serves: 3

IMPERIAL	METRIC	AMERICAN
3 shallots *or* baby onions	3 shallots *or* baby onions	3 shallots *or* baby onions
1½ oz. butter	40 g. butter	3 tablespoons butter
6 tablespoons dry white wine	6 tablespoons dry white wine	½ cup dry white wine
2 tablespoons concentrated meat stock	2 tablespoons concentrated meat stock	3 tablespoons concentrated meat stock
1 tablespoon chopped parsley	1 tablespoon chopped parsley	1 tablespoon chopped parsley
1–2 teaspoons lemon juice	1–2 teaspoons lemon juice	1–2 teaspoons lemon juice

Chop the shallots or onions *very* finely. Melt half the butter in a small saucepan and fry the shallots gently until soft but uncoloured. Add the wine and bubble briskly until reduced by half. Add the stock. Off the heat, beat in the remaining butter, the parsley and lemon juice to taste.

Serve with: fried or grilled liver, chops, eggs or sausages.

Variation

Sauce bercy for fish
Substitute concentrated fish stock for the meat stock and serve with grilled or baked fish fillets.

Cumberland rum butter

Serves: 4

IMPERIAL	METRIC	AMERICAN
2 oz. butter	50 g. butter	¼ cup butter
2 oz. soft brown sugar	50 g. soft brown sugar	¼ cup soft brown sugar, firmly packed
½ teaspoon grated lemon rind *or* pinch each nutmeg and cinnamon	½ teaspoon grated lemon rind *or* pinch each nutmeg and cinnamon	½ teaspoon grated lemon rind *or* pinch each nutmeg and cinnamon
2–3 tablespoons rum	2–3 tablespoons rum	3–4 tablespoons rum

Cream the butter thoroughly, beat in the sugar and lemon rind or spices. Then gradually beat in enough rum to flavour strongly.

Serve with: baked apples or bananas, steamed fruit puddings, mince pies, or use as a cake filling.

Paradise dressing

Cooking time: about 15 minutes

IMPERIAL	METRIC	AMERICAN
1 tablespoon chopped onion	1 tablespoon chopped onion	1 tablespoon chopped onion
1 tablespoon vegetable oil	1 tablespoon vegetable oil	1 tablespoon vegetable oil
1½ teaspoons curry powder	1½ teaspoons curry powder	1½ teaspoons curry powder
2 tablespoons red wine	2 tablespoons red wine	3 tablespoons red wine
1 teaspoon lemon juice	1 teaspoon lemon juice	1 teaspoon lemon juice
1 tablespoon apricot purée	1 tablespoon apricot purée	1 tablespoon apricot purée
¼ pint mayonnaise*	1½ dl. mayonnaise*	⅔ cup mayonnaise*
salt, pepper and paprika	salt, pepper and paprika	salt, pepper and paprika

Chop the onion very finely and in a small saucepan fry gently in the oil until soft but uncoloured. Add the curry powder and cook over low heat for a few minutes. Stir in the red wine, lemon juice and apricot purée and allow to bubble briskly for a few minutes until well reduced. Cool the mixture, and when cold stir into the mayonnaise with seasonings to taste.
*If using ordinary bottled mayonnaise, stir in about 2 tablespoons double cream to mellow the flavour. Use for: dressing fruit salads, chicken or fish salads.

Chicken liver sauce

Cooking time: 45 minutes
Serves: 4

IMPERIAL	METRIC	AMERICAN
1½ oz. butter	40 g. butter	3 tablespoons butter
2 oz. unsmoked streaky bacon, chopped	50 g. unsmoked streaky bacon, chopped	3 slices unsmoked bacon, chopped
1 small onion, finely chopped	1 small onion, finely chopped	1 small onion, finely chopped
2 oz. mushrooms, finely chopped	50 g. mushrooms, finely chopped	½ cup finely chopped mushrooms
8 oz. chicken livers	225 g. chicken livers	½ lb. chicken livers
1 tablespoon flour	1 tablespoon flour	1 tablespoon flour
2 tablespoons Marsala *or* medium sweet sherry	2 tablespoons Marsala *or* medium sweet sherry	3 tablespoons Marsala *or* medium sweet sherry
1 tablespoon tomato purée	1 tablespoon tomato purée	1 tablespoon tomato paste
½ pint chicken stock	3 dl. chicken stock	1¼ cups chicken stock
salt and pepper	salt and pepper	salt and pepper

Put 1 oz. butter, the bacon, onion and mushrooms into a saucepan and cook over *gentle* heat for 10 minutes. Chop the livers finely, having first discarded any tissues or discoloured parts. Add the livers and flour to the vegetables, increase the heat and stir for a minute or two until the livers change colour.

Add the wine and bubble briskly until almost evaporated, then stir in the tomato purée followed by the stock. Add seasoning to taste, cover, and simmer gently for about 30 minutes. Stir in the remaining butter.

Serve with: any type of egg pasta, and especially green noodles, potato gnocchi or boiled rice.

Fresh strawberry or raspberry sauce

Serves: 4

IMPERIAL	METRIC	AMERICAN
1 lb. raspberries *or* strawberries	450 g. raspberries *or* strawberries	1 lb. raspberries *or* strawberries
about 2 oz. icing sugar	about 50 g. icing sugar	about ½ cup confectioners' sugar
very little Kirsch *or* Cointreau	very little Kirsch *or* Cointreau	very little Kirsch *or* Cointreau

Sieve the fruit, ideally by rubbing through a nylon strainer as this removes all seeds and pips. (If you do not mind the pips use an electric blender or simply mash the fruit very thoroughly.) Beat in the sugar gradually. Flavour with liqueur, starting with one teaspoonful; tasting as you go.

Serve with: vanilla ice cream, poached pears or peaches.

Marsala or Madeira foam sauce

Cooking time: about 10 minutes
Serves: 3–4

IMPERIAL	METRIC	AMERICAN
¼ pint Marsala *or* dry Madeira	1½ dl. Marsala *or* dry Madeira	⅔ cup Marsala *or* dry Madeira
3 tablespoons water	3 tablespoons water	¼ cup water
3 tablespoons castor sugar	3 tablespoons castor sugar	¼ cup granulated sugar
3 egg yolks	3 egg yolks	3 egg yolks
for cold sauce only	*for cold sauce only*	*for cold sauce only*
4 tablespoons double cream	4 tablespoons double cream	⅓ cup whipping cream

A rich and sweet sauce. Put all the ingredients in the top half of a double boiler and whisk over boiling water until the sauce becomes a thick foam. Immediately remove from the heat as overcooking will cause the sauce to curdle.

Transfer to a jug and either serve at once or stand in a pan of warm, not boiling, water until required.

To serve cold: allow sauce to cool, whisking from time to time. When cold, stir in double cream.

Serve hot with: steamed plum pudding, raisin or canary pudding.

Serve cold with: fresh strawberries, poached fresh peaches or pears.

Fish

In traditional French cooking, fish cooked 'au vin blanc' is one of the most basic of basic recipes. You find it frequently among the practical dishes a housewife prepares for her family, using a local vin ordinaire. In other countries use an inexpensive medium dry white wine such as you are likely to find under the names of Mâcon, Graves, Entre-deux-Mers, Bordeaux or Spanish Chablis. If the only wine you have is dry and thin, try rounding out the flavour with a tablespoon or two of sweet white vermouth. Dry cider, too, is excellent for cooking fish; you can use it in place of white wine in any fish dish.

Red wines are sometimes used too, especially for salmon, sole, and in matelotes (type of fish stew) of eel or fresh water fish. It should, however, be a full bodied red wine.

The recipes in this chapter use the types of fish most generally available and, apart from one or two exceptions, are of an everyday rather than a special occasion nature. Many of the recipes are based on ready filleted fish which are available frozen as well as fresh.

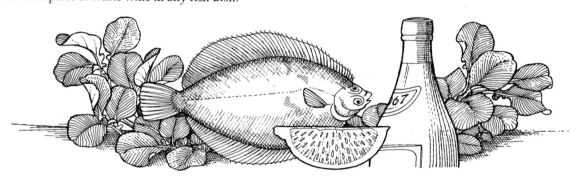

Baked halibut Sicilian style

Cooking time: 25–30 minutes
Temperature: 375°F., 190°C.,
   Gas Mark 5
Serves: 4

IMPERIAL	METRIC	AMERICAN
1¼–1½ lb. halibut steaks	600–700 g. halibut steaks	1¼–1½ lb. halibut steaks
2 tablespoons olive oil	2 tablespoons olive oil	3 tablespoons olive oil
1 large onion, chopped	1 large onion, chopped	1 large onion, chopped
1 stick celery, chopped	1 stick celery, chopped	1 stalk celery, chopped
4 ripe tomatoes, peeled and quartered	4 ripe tomatoes, peeled and quartered	4 ripe tomatoes, peeled and quartered
6 tablespoons medium dry white wine	6 tablespoons medium dry white wine	½ cup medium dry white wine
2 tablespoons water	2 tablespoons water	3 tablespoons water
salt, pepper and sugar	salt, pepper and sugar	salt, pepper and sugar
12 green olives, stoned and chopped	12 green olives, stoned and chopped	12 green olives, pitted and chopped
1 tablespoon capers	1 tablespoon capers	1 tablespoon capers
1 tablespoon chopped fresh parsley	1 tablespoon chopped fresh parsley	1 tablespoon chopped fresh parsley

Wipe the fish, cut into portions and arrange in a buttered shallow heatproof dish. Heat the oil and over gentle heat fry the onion and celery until soft but uncoloured, about 5 minutes. De-seed the tomatoes and add the chopped flesh to the pan with the wine and water, season with salt, pepper and sugar.

Stir until boiling and simmer for 5 minutes. Add the olives and capers and pour over the fish. Bake in centre of the preheated oven, basting occasionally. Sprinkle with the parsley and serve hot in the same dish.

Fillets of fish à la crème (see recipe on page 32)

Mackerel in white wine

Cooking time: 20 minutes
Temperature: 375°F., 190°C.,
   Gas Mark 5
Serves: 4

IMPERIAL	METRIC	AMERICAN
4 small fresh mackerel	4 small fresh mackerel	4 small fresh mackerel
½ oz. butter	15 g. butter	1 tablespoon butter
1 small carrot, thinly sliced	1 small carrot, thinly sliced	1 small carrot, thinly sliced
2 small onions, thinly sliced	2 small onions, thinly sliced	2 small onions, thinly sliced
2 slices lemon	2 slices lemon	2 slices lemon
salt	salt	salt
ground black pepper	ground black pepper	ground black pepper
½ pint dry white wine	3 dl. dry white wine	1¼ cups dry white wine
1 tablespoon chopped herbs (parsley, chervil and chives)	1 tablespoon chopped herbs (parsley, chervil and chives)	1 tablespoon chopped herbs (parsley, chervil and chives)

Mackerel are excellent cooked this way, for a meal starter or supper dish. Clean and wash the mackerel. Butter a shallow ovenproof dish and strew the carrot, onions and lemon over the base. Arrange the fish on top. Sprinkle with salt and pepper, and pour the wine over. Scatter the herbs on top. Cook in the preheated oven for 20 minutes, basting now and then.

Leave to cool in the liquid, and serve when cold. For an elegant meal the cooked mackerel can be skinned and filleted, covered with the strained and reduced cooking liquor, and sprinkled with chopped fresh herbs.

Variation
Herring in white wine
Fresh herring cooked exactly as above.

Creamed salmon and shrimp gratin

Cooking time: 15–20 minutes
Temperature: 425°F., 220°C.,
   Gas Mark 7
Serves: 4

IMPERIAL	METRIC	AMERICAN
1½ oz. butter	40 g. butter	3 tablespoons butter
1 oz. finely chopped onion	25 g. finely chopped onion	¼ cup finely chopped onion
1½ oz. flour	40 g. flour	6 tablespoons flour
½ pint hot milk	3 dl. hot milk	1¼ cups hot milk
4 tablespoons dry white wine *or* dry vermouth	4 tablespoons dry white wine *or* dry vermouth	⅓ cup dry white wine *or* dry vermouth
salt and pepper	salt and pepper	salt and pepper
3–4 tablespoons thick cream	3–4 tablespoons thick cream	¼–⅓ cup whipping cream
6 oz. cooked *or* canned salmon, flaked	175 g. cooked *or* canned salmon, flaked	1½ cups flaked cooked *or* canned salmon
2 oz. peeled shrimps *or* prawns	50 g. peeled shrimps *or* prawns	⅓ cup shelled shrimp *or* prawns
2 sliced hard-boiled eggs	2 sliced hard-boiled eggs	2 sliced hard-cooked eggs
1 oz. finely grated cheese	25 g. finely grated cheese	¼ cup finely grated cheese

Melt the butter in a saucepan and cook the onion gently until soft but uncoloured, about 5 minutes. Stir in the flour and cook for 2 minutes, stirring all the time. Off the heat add the milk, wine and seasoning and bring rapidly to the boil whisking all the time until the sauce thickens. Fold in the cream, salmon, shrimps or prawns and hard-boiled egg.

Turn into a buttered gratin dish and sprinkle evenly with cheese. Bake towards top of the preheated oven for 15 minutes or until lightly browned.
Note. Divided between 4 individual dishes this makes a pleasant first course.

Cod or haddock steaks duglère

Cooking time: 20–25 minutes
Serves: 2–4

IMPERIAL	METRIC	AMERICAN
1 oz. butter	25 g. butter	2 tablespoons butter
1 medium onion, finely chopped	1 medium onion, finely chopped	1 medium onion, finely chopped
3 ripe tomatoes, skinned and de-seeded	3 ripe tomatoes, skinned and de-seeded	3 ripe tomatoes, skinned and de-seeded
1 tablespoon chopped parsley	1 tablespoon chopped parsley	1 tablespoon chopped parsley
6 tablespoons dry white wine	6 tablespoons dry white wine	½ cup dry white wine
4 tablespoons water	4 tablespoons water	⅓ cup water
salt and pepper	salt and pepper	salt and pepper
14 oz. frozen cod or haddock steaks	400 g. frozen cod or haddock steaks	14 oz. frozen cod or haddock steaks
½ oz. butter	15 g. butter	1 tablespoon butter
½ oz. flour	15 g. flour	2 tablespoons flour
sprigs of parsley	sprigs of parsley	sprigs of parsley

Melt the butter in a wide saucepan and over low heat fry the onion until soft but uncoloured. Add the tomatoes, parsley, wine, water and seasoning, and bring to the boil. Put the haddock steaks into the pan, cover and poach very gently for 15 to 20 minutes.

Cream together the butter and flour. Remove the cooked fish and arrange on a serving dish. To the saucepan add the creamed butter and flour in small pieces, whisking continuously, until the sauce thickens. Check the seasoning then pour over the fish. Garnish with the parsley and serve with creamy mashed potato.

Red mullet Venetian style

Cooking time: 10–15 minutes
Serves: 4

IMPERIAL	METRIC	AMERICAN
four 8-oz. or two 1-lb. red mullet	four 225-g. or two 450-g. red mullet	four ½-lb. or two 1-lb. red mullet
several garlic cloves	several garlic cloves	several garlic cloves
few mint leaves	few mint leaves	few mint leaves
salt	salt	salt
olive oil for frying	olive oil for frying	olive oil for frying
2 tablespoons finely chopped onion	2 tablespoons finely chopped onion	3 tablespoons finely chopped onion
¼ pint medium dry white wine	1½ dl. medium dry white wine	⅔ cup medium dry white wine
1 tablespoon wine vinegar	1 tablespoon wine vinegar	1 tablespoon wine vinegar
orange and lemon slices	orange and lemon slices	orange and lemon slices

Ask the fishmonger to gut and scale the mullet but leave the heads on. Put one crushed clove of garlic and two bruised mint leaves inside each cavity. Make two small incisions across the flesh on each side of the fish, rub lightly with salt and then with oil. Put under a medium hot grill and cook steadily for 5 to 7 minutes each side, depending on size.

Meanwhile, fry the chopped onion very gently in 2 tablespoons of oil, when soft add the wine and vinegar and simmer for 10 minutes. When cold pour over the mullet and leave to marinate for several hours. Serve garnished with orange and lemon slices.

Salmon steaks in white wine

Cooking time: 25–30 minutes
Serves: 4

IMPERIAL	METRIC	AMERICAN
4 salmon steaks, about $\frac{3}{4}$ inch thick	4 salmon steaks, about 2 cm. thick	4 salmon steaks, about $\frac{3}{4}$ inch thick
little seasoned flour	little seasoned flour	little seasoned flour
2 oz. butter	50 g. butter	$\frac{1}{4}$ cup butter
1 tablespoon olive oil	1 tablespoon olive oil	1 tablespoon olive oil
$\frac{1}{3}$ pint dry white wine	2 dl. dry white wine	scant 1 cup dry white wine
2 bay leaves	2 bay leaves	2 bay leaves
large pinch celery seed	large pinch celery seed	large pinch celery seed
lemon slices	lemon slices	lemon slices
chopped parsley	chopped parsley	chopped parsley

Coat the salmon steaks with seasoned flour. Heat the butter and oil in a wide pan with lid and fry the steaks gently until golden on both sides, about 10 minutes. Pour over the wine and add bay leaves and celery seed.

Cover the pan, and cook very gently, basting frequently for 15 to 20 minutes. Dish the steaks, check the pan juices for seasoning and pour over. Garnish with lemon slices dipped in chopped parsley.

Sailors' risotto

Cooking time: 40 minutes
Serves: 4

IMPERIAL	METRIC	AMERICAN
3 oz. butter	75 g. butter	6 tablespoons butter
3 oz. onion, finely chopped	75 g. onion, finely chopped	1 small onion, finely chopped
1 stick celery, finely chopped	1 stick celery, finely chopped	1 stalk celery, finely chopped
12 oz. round grain rice, preferably Italian	350 g. round grain rice, preferably Italian	$1\frac{3}{4}$ cups short grain rice, preferably Italian
6 tablespoons dry white wine	6 tablespoons dry white wine	$\frac{1}{2}$ cup dry white wine
$1\frac{1}{2}$–2 pints hot fish stock*	about 1 litre hot fish stock*	4–5 cups hot fish stock*
$\frac{1}{2}$ pint fresh prawns	3 dl. fresh prawns	$1\frac{1}{4}$ cups fresh shrimp or prawns
8 oz. lobster meat, fresh or canned	225 g. lobster meat, fresh or canned	$1\frac{1}{2}$ cups lobster meat, fresh or canned
1 oz. grated Parmesan cheese	25 g. grated Parmesan cheese	$\frac{1}{4}$ cup grated Parmesan cheese
2 pints fresh mussels, scrubbed	generous 1 litre fresh mussels, scrubbed	5 cups fresh mussels, scrubbed
1 tablespoon chopped parsley	1 tablespoon chopped parsley	1 tablespoon chopped parsley

Heat half the butter in a saucepan over low heat and fry onion and celery for 5 minutes. Add rice and stir until translucent, then add wine and cook until almost evaporated. Add hot stock in 3 or 4 instalments, adding more as the previous addition is absorbed. Cook uncovered over a medium heat, stirring frequently. Reserve some of the prawns for garnish and peel the remainder. Cut lobster meat into bite-size pieces and heat through gently with the prawns in the remaining butter; add to the risotto with the final addition of stock and grated cheese. Put the scrubbed and bearded mussels, using only those with tightly closed shells, into a large rinsed saucepan and shake over brisk heat until they open, about 5 to 10 minutes. Pile the risotto on to a serving dish and garnish with the reserved prawns, parsley and mussels in shells.

Note. Vongole (small clams) or cockles can be used in the risotto and are prepared in the same way as mussels.

*Prepare fish stock by simmering lobster and prawn shells in water to cover with a sliced onion, stick of celery, salt and bay leaf for one hour; strain.

Beefsteak with wine sauce (see recipe on page 40)

Fillets of fish à la crème

(illustrated on page 27)
Cooking time: 15–20 minutes
Temperature: 350°F., 180°C.,
  Gas Mark 4
Serves: 4

IMPERIAL	METRIC	AMERICAN
1 small onion *or* shallot	1 small onion *or* shallot	1 small onion *or* shallot
1½ lb. skinned fish fillets*	700 g. skinned fish fillets*	1½ lb. skinned fish fillets*
salt and pepper	salt and pepper	salt and pepper
¼ pint dry white wine	1½ dl. dry white wine	⅔ cup dry white wine
¼ pint water	1½ dl. water	⅔ cup water
½ oz. butter	15 g. butter	1 tablespoon butter
½ oz. flour	15 g. flour	2 tablespoons flour
¼ pint double cream	1½ dl. double cream	⅔ cup whipping cream
few black grapes	few black grapes	few purple grapes
squeeze of lemon juice	squeeze of lemon juice	squeeze of lemon juice
1 oz. finely grated Parmesan cheese (optional)	25 g. finely grated Parmesan cheese (optional)	¼ cup finely grated Parmesan cheese (optional)

Chop the onion or shallot very finely and sprinkle over the bottom of a buttered shallow heatproof dish. Lay the fish fillets skinned-side down on top. Season, and pour in the wine and water. Cover lightly with buttered greaseproof paper. Cook towards top of the preheated oven for 15 to 20 minutes depending on thickness of fillets.

Cream together the butter and flour. When the fish is cooked drain the poaching liquid into a saucepan and boil furiously until reduced to ¼ pint. Remove from the heat, beat in the creamed butter and flour and when smooth stir in the cream. Bring to the boil, stirring all the time, and if too thick thin down with a little milk. Add the halved and deseeded grapes and lemon juice, check the seasoning and pour over the folded fillets. If liked, sprinkle with cheese and slip the dish under a preheated grill for 2 to 3 minutes until golden.

*Any firm-fleshed fish such as halibut, flounder, turbot or sole.

Lobster Newburg

Cooking time: 10–12 minutes
Serves: 3–4

IMPERIAL	METRIC	AMERICAN
12 oz. cooked lobster meat	350 g. cooked lobster meat	2 cups cooked lobster meat
1 oz. butter	25 g. butter	2 tablespoons butter
5 tablespoons dry Madeira *or* medium dry sherry	5 tablespoons dry Madeira *or* medium dry sherry	6 tablespoons dry Madeira *or* medium dry sherry
2 egg yolks	2 egg yolks	2 egg yolks
⅓ pint double cream	2 dl. double cream	scant 1 cup whipping cream
salt and ground black pepper	salt and ground black pepper	salt and ground black pepper
shake of cayenne	shake of cayenne	shake of cayenne
8 oz. cooked long grain rice (3 oz. raw rice) *or* 4 rounds buttered toast	225 g. cooked long grain rice (75 g. raw rice) *or* 4 rounds buttered toast	1½ cups cooked long grain rice (½ cup raw rice) *or* 4 rounds buttered toast
shake of paprika	shake of paprika	shake of paprika

Cut the lobster into bite-size pieces and heat *gently* in the melted butter for 5 minutes. Add the wine and increase the heat so that the wine is reduced by half. Remove from the heat. Beat the egg yolks with the cream and seasoning and add to the lobster. Stir gently to mix.

Replace over *very low* heat and shake and tip the pan gently all the time until the sauce thickens. Remove from heat at once. Do not overheat or curdling may result; if in any doubt, thicken the sauce in the top half of a double boiler over boiling water. Check seasoning, and serve on rice or toast and garnish with a light sprinkling of paprika.

Variations
Scampi or crab Newburg
Use 12 oz. scampi or cooked crab instead of lobster.

Coquilles St. Jacques à la provençale

Cooking time: 10–12 minutes
Serves: 4

IMPERIAL	METRIC	AMERICAN
6 large or 8 small scallops	6 large or 8 small scallops	1 lb. large fresh scallops
1½ oz. butter	40 g. butter	3 tablespoons butter
1 tablespoon chopped onion or shallot	1 tablespoon chopped onion or shallot	1 tablespoon chopped onion or shallot
1 small garlic clove, crushed	1 small garlic clove, crushed	1 small garlic clove, crushed
2 tablespoons seasoned flour	2 tablespoons seasoned flour	3 tablespoons seasoned flour
6 tablespoons dry white wine	6 tablespoons dry white wine	½ cup dry white wine
¼ bay leaf	¼ bay leaf	¼ bay leaf
pinch of powdered thyme	pinch of powdered thyme	pinch of powdered thyme
mashed potato (optional)	mashed potato (optional)	mashed potato (optional)

Ask the fishmonger to clean the scallops and give you the deep shells for serving them in. Melt the butter in a saucepan and over *low* heat fry the onion or shallot until soft but uncoloured. Add the garlic and cook for a moment or two. Meanwhile, separate the orange roes and cut the scallops horizontally in half. Toss all in seasoned flour. Put into the pan with the onions and cook gently for 5 to 6 minutes, turning now and then to cook evenly right through. Transfer to 4 clean and warmed deep shells.

Add the wine and herbs to the pan, stir the base of the pan to scrape up all the juices, and boil rapidly until well reduced and slightly thickened. Discard bay leaf and spoon sauce over scallops. If liked, pipe a border of mashed potato around each. Serve immediately.

Note. If more convenient these scallops can be prepared a few hours in advance. Just before serving sprinkle with grated cheese, dot with butter and put under a moderate grill for 3 to 4 minutes to heat through and brown lightly.

Fish fillets au gratin

Cooking time: about 20 minutes
Temperature: 400°F., 200°C., Gas Mark 6
Serves: 4

IMPERIAL	METRIC	AMERICAN
2 oz. butter	50 g. butter	¼ cup butter
1 tablespoon finely chopped onion	1 tablespoon finely chopped onion	1 tablespoon finely chopped onion
4 oz. mushrooms, finely chopped	100 g. mushrooms, finely chopped	1 cup finely chopped mushrooms
¼ pint medium dry white wine	1½ dl. medium dry white wine	⅔ cup medium dry white wine
1¼ lb. white fish fillets – haddock, turbot, etc.	600 g. white fish fillets, – haddock, turbot, etc.	1¼ lb. white fish fillets – haddock, turbot, etc.
salt and pepper	salt and pepper	salt and pepper
3 tablespoons fresh breadcrumbs	3 tablespoons fresh breadcrumbs	¼ cup fresh bread crumbs
1 tablespoon chopped parsley	1 tablespoon chopped parsley	1 tablespoon chopped parsley

Melt half the butter and fry onion over *low* heat until soft but not coloured. Add mushrooms and cook for 1 minute. Add wine and boil rapidly for another minute. Meanwhile lay fish fillets in a buttered shallow ovenproof dish, season and pour the wine mixture over them. Sprinkle evenly with breadcrumbs and dot with remaining butter.

Cook near the top of the preheated oven for about 20 minutes, until fish is just cooked and crumbs golden and crisp. Sprinkle with parsley, and serve hot in same dish.

Poultry and game

The bland flavour of poultry responds most favourably to the addition of wine and herbs, and sometimes cream as well. In France both red and white wine feature prominently in chicken dishes, usually a good local wine, and the dish is named accordingly. So in Arbois you may find 'Poulet sauté au vin jaune' and travelling west into the Burgundy area 'Coq au beaujolais' or 'Coq au chambertin'.

Dry white vermouth is an excellent substitute for white wine, adding a pleasant herby flavour at the same time; as it is stronger you need use only about half as much. Fortified wines, too, combine excellently with poultry, and a medium dry variety of sherry, Madeira, Marsala or port can be used to good effect.

For town dwellers game, alas, is scarce and expensive, but some recipes have been included for both young and casserole birds. To compete with the stronger flavour of game, and this includes hare, the robust red wines are usually the more successful, port is good, and brandy never comes amiss. But as always with wine and food the most unlikely combinations can be winners, so don't be afraid to experiment.

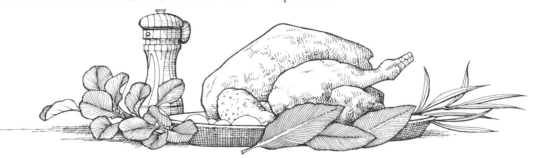

Rabbit pâté

Cooking time: about 1½ hours
Temperature: 325°F., 170°C.,
  Gas Mark 3
Serves: 8

IMPERIAL	METRIC	AMERICAN
2 lb. rabbit, weighed after skinning	1 kg. rabbit, weighed after skinning	2 lb. rabbit, weighed after skinning
12 oz. pork sausage meat	350 g. pork sausage meat	¾ lb. pork sausage meat
½ garlic clove, crushed	½ garlic clove, crushed	½ garlic clove, crushed
3–4 oz. *thin* rashers unsmoked streaky bacon	75–100 g. *thin* rashers unsmoked streaky bacon	4–5 *thin* slices unsmoked bacon
marinade	*marinade*	*marinade*
2 tablespoons brandy	2 tablespoons brandy	3 tablespoons brandy
3 tablespoons red *or* white wine	3 tablespoons red *or* white wine	¼ cup red *or* white wine
½ tablespoon wine vinegar	½ tablespoon wine vinegar	½ tablespoon wine vinegar
1 onion, sliced	1 onion, sliced	1 onion, sliced
1 bay leaf, sprig of thyme and parsley tied	1 bay leaf, sprig of thyme and parsley, tied	1 bay leaf, sprig of thyme and parsley, tied
salt and ground black pepper	salt and ground black pepper	salt and ground black pepper

Joint and bone the rabbit. Slice the meat into strips about ½ inch wide. Put into a china basin with all the ingredients of the marinade. Stir well, cover, and leave in a cool place for 6 to 12 hours, stirring occasionally.

Chop the heart and liver and mix with the sausage meat, garlic and strained liquid from the marinade.

Line a 2-pint terrine or deep pie dish with the bacon and in it arrange alternate layers of sausage meat and rabbit. Top with bacon rashers. Cover with lid or foil, place in a baking tin with hot water to reach half way up the dish, and bake in the centre of a preheated oven for about 1½ hours. Press with a weight while cooling. Turn out and serve cold, in slices, with salad.

Casseroled pheasant with chestnuts and celery

Cooking time: about 1¾ hours
Temperature: 325°F., 170°F.,
　　Gas Mark 3
Serves: 3–4

IMPERIAL	METRIC	AMERICAN
6 oz. chestnuts	175 g. chestnuts	2 cups chestnuts
1 oz. butter	25 g. butter	2 tablespoons butter
1 casserole pheasant, dressed for oven	1 casserole pheasant, dressed for oven	1 casserole pheasant, dressed for oven
4 oz. button onions, peeled	100 g. button onions, peeled	about 8 tiny onions, peeled
6 sticks celery, cut in 1½-inch lengths	6 sticks celery, cut in 4-cm. lengths	6 stalks celery, cut in 1½-inch lengths
1 oz. flour	25 g. flour	¼ cup flour
¼ pint robust red wine	1½ dl. robust red wine	⅔ cup robust red wine
½ pint stock	3 dl. stock	1¼ cups stock
2 teaspoons redcurrant jelly	2 teaspoons redcurrant jelly	2 teaspoons red currant jelly
2 thin strips orange rind	2 thin strips orange rind	2 thin strips orange rind
1 small bay leaf	1 small bay leaf	1 small bay leaf
salt and pepper	salt and pepper	salt and pepper

Cut a slit in the skin of each chestnut, spread on a baking sheet and cook in a moderately hot oven for 10–15 minutes. When cool enough to handle remove the outer and inner skins. Melt the butter in a heatproof casserole and then brown the pheasant slowly on all sides; remove from the pan. Add the chestnuts, onion and celery and fry gently for 5 minutes. Sprinkle in the flour and stir until the remaining fat is absorbed. Stir in the wine, stock, jelly, orange rind, bay leaf, and seasoning to taste. Bring to the boil.

Put in the pheasant breast downwards, cover tightly, and cook in the centre of the preheated oven for about 1½ hours or until tender, turning at half time. Dish the pheasant and surround with chestnuts, onions and celery. Discard bay leaf and orange rind, if necessary reduce the sauce by boiling rapidly for a few minutes. Check seasoning. Pour some sauce over pheasant and serve the rest separately.

Pheasant with apples and cream

Cooking time: 1 hour
Serves: 3

IMPERIAL	METRIC	AMERICAN
1 oz. butter	25 g. butter	2 tablespoons butter
1 tablespoon oil	1 tablespoon oil	1 tablespoon oil
1 young pheasant, oven-ready	1 young pheasant, oven-ready	1 young pheasant, oven-ready
3 oz. finely chopped onion	75 g. finely chopped onion	½ cup finely chopped onion
3 tablespoons Calvados or brandy	3 tablespoons Calvados or brandy	¼ cup Calvados or brandy
¼ pint game or chicken stock	1½ dl. game or chicken stock	⅔ cup game or chicken stock
8 oz. dessert apples, peeled, cored and sliced	225 g. dessert apples, peeled, cored and sliced	2 medium dessert apples, peeled, cored and sliced
¼ pint double cream	1½ dl. double cream	⅔ cup whipping cream
salt and pepper	salt and pepper	salt and pepper
apple rings fried in butter	apple rings fried in butter	apple rings fried in butter

Heat butter and oil in a flameproof casserole and slowly brown pheasant all over. Cook onion at the same time. Drain off surplus fat. Pour Calvados or brandy into a heated ladle, set alight and pour over pheasant. When flames die, add the stock, apples, cream and seasoning. Cover tightly and simmer very gently for about 40 to 50 minutes.

Remove pheasant, carve and arrange on serving dish. Press sauce through a strainer, return to pan and boil rapidly until reduced to coating consistency. Check seasoning and pour over pheasant. Garnish with fried apple rings.

Coq au vin rouge

(illustrated on front cover)
Cooking time: 1½ hours
Temperature: 350°F., 180°C.,
Gas Mark 4
Serves: 4

IMPERIAL	METRIC	AMERICAN
3-lb. chicken, jointed *or* quartered	1½-kg. chicken, jointed *or* quartered	3-lb. chicken, jointed *or* quartered
1 small onion, sliced	1 small onion, sliced	1 small onion, sliced
salt and ground black pepper	salt and ground black pepper	salt and ground black pepper
4 oz. unsmoked streaky bacon	100 g. unsmoked streaky bacon	5 slices unsmoked bacon
1½ oz. butter	40 g. butter	3 tablespoons butter
1 tablespoon olive oil	1 tablespoon olive oil	1 tablespoon olive oil
12 button onions, peeled	12 button onions, peeled	12 tiny onions, peeled
1 garlic clove, crushed	1 garlic clove, crushed	1 garlic clove, crushed
bouquet of bay leaf, thyme and parsley, tied	bouquet of bay leaf, thyme and parsley, tied	bouquet of bay leaf, thyme and parsley, tied
2 tablespoons brandy	2 tablespoons brandy	3 tablespoons brandy
½ bottle red wine, preferably Burgundy	½ bottle red wine, preferably Burgundy	½ bottle red wine, preferably Burgundy
4 oz. button mushrooms	100 g. button mushrooms	1 cup button mushrooms
1 oz. flour	25 g. flour	¼ cup flour
1 oz. softened butter	25 g. softened butter	2 tablespoons softened butter
crescents of bread fried crisp in butter	crescents of bread fried crisp in butter	crescents of bread fried crisp in butter

This famous dish well repays the extra attention needed while cooking. Remove backbone and leg shanks from chicken and simmer for 30 minutes with the giblets, onion, seasoning, and water just to cover. Strain and reserve stock.

Cut bacon into ¼-inch strips and dry chicken pieces. Heat butter and oil in a wide sauté pan, add chicken joints, bacon and onions, and fry briskly, turning as necessary, until golden, about 12 minutes. Add the garlic, herbs and seasoning, cover, and cook over *low* heat for 10 minutes. Drain off surplus fat. Pour brandy into a heated ladle, ignite and pour over chicken. Shake pan gently until flames die down. Add wine and stock, when boiling cover pan tightly, transfer to centre of preheated oven for 1 hour. Remove chicken and keep warm. Discard herbs. Boil liquid rapidly until reduced to about ½ pint. Cream flour and butter to a paste (this is the French beurre manié, used for thickening liquids) and add to the pan in walnut-size pieces, whisking briskly all the time until sauce is medium thick. Check seasoning, add mushrooms and replace chicken. Heat gently for 10 minutes. Serve from casserole or arrange in a shallow dish and garnish with the croûtons. Serve with plain boiled potatoes tossed in butter and chopped parsley. Drink a wine similar to the one used in the cooking.

Note. Coq au vin can also be made with white wine. When a special wine is used the dish takes the name of the wine, for example Coq au Chambertin or Coq au Riesling.

Roast grouse with grapes

Cooking time: 30 minutes
Temperature: 400°F., 200°C.,
Gas Mark 6
Serves: 4

IMPERIAL	METRIC	AMERICAN
8 oz. white grapes	225 g. white grapes	½ lb. green grapes
2 oz. butter	50 g. butter	¼ cup butter
2 young grouse, ready for the oven	2 young grouse, ready for the oven	2 young grouse, ready for the oven
6 thin rashers fat unsmoked bacon	6 thin rashers fat unsmoked bacon	6 thin slices unsmoked bacon
¼ pint port	1½ dl. port	⅔ cup port
4 slices bread fried in butter	4 slices bread fried in butter	4 slices bread fried in butter

Skin and de-seed the grapes. Insert a walnut of butter and 4 to 7 grapes inside each grouse. Smear the rest of the butter all over the birds, and lay the rashers of bacon over the breasts. Place on a rack in a roasting tin and cook in the preheated oven for 20 minutes. Pour the warmed port over the birds and continue roasting for another 10 minutes, basting several times. Put the remaining grapes in the oven to warm.

Remove the birds, and discard bacon. Cut each bird in half and lay cut-side down on a slice of fried bread. Reduce liquor in the roasting tin by rapid boiling; check seasoning and pour over the birds. Serve with the grapes and some hot straw potatoes.

Chicken Marengo

(illustrated on page 23)
Cooking time: about 1 hour
Serves: 4

IMPERIAL	METRIC	AMERICAN
2-lb. roasting chicken, jointed, *or* 4 chicken quarters	1-kg. roasting chicken, jointed, *or* 4 chicken quarters	2-lb. roasting chicken, jointed, *or* 4 chicken quarters
3 tablespoons oil	3 tablespoons oil	¼ cup oil
1 small onion, chopped	1 small onion, chopped	1 small onion, chopped
1 garlic clove, crushed	1 garlic clove, crushed	1 garlic clove, crushed
2 tablespoons flour	2 tablespoons flour	3 tablespoons flour
¼ pint medium dry wine	1½ dl. medium dry wine	⅔ cup medium dry wine
½ pint chicken stock	3 dl. chicken stock	1¼ cups chicken stock
1 tablespoon thick tomato purée	1 tablespoon thick tomato purée	1 tablespoon thick tomato paste
salt and pepper	salt and pepper	salt and pepper
4 oz. button mushrooms	100 g. button mushrooms	1 cup button mushrooms
chopped fresh parsley *or* heart-shaped croûtons	chopped fresh parsley *or* heart-shaped croûtons	chopped fresh parsley *or* heart-shaped croûtons

This famous dish is said to have been invented by Napoleon's chef to celebrate the victory at Marengo when the only ingredients available on the battlefield were some scraggy chicken, wine, oil and mushrooms.

Heat the oil in a heatproof casserole, and over gentle heat fry the chicken joints until golden brown all over. Add the onion and garlic and fry with the chicken. Stir in the flour and cook for a minute, then stir in the wine, chicken stock and tomato purée. Add the button mushrooms, then cover the pan closely and simmer gently for about 40 minutes. Dish the chicken, reduce the sauce by boiling if necessary, and pour over chicken. Garnish with freshly chopped parsley or croûtons of fried bread. If liked, serve with boiled rice.

Sauté of chicken livers

Cooking time: 7–8 minutes
Serves: 4

IMPERIAL	METRIC	AMERICAN
12 oz. chicken livers	350 g. chicken livers	¾ lb. chicken livers
½ oz. seasoned flour	15 g. seasoned flour	1 tablespoon seasoned flour
2-oz. rasher gammon	50-g. rasher gammon	1 thick slice Canadian-style bacon
2 oz. butter	50 g. butter	¼ cup butter
2 tablespoons Madeira *or* sherry	2 tablespoons Madeira *or* sherry	3 tablespoons Madeira *or* sherry
5–6 tablespoons stock *or* water	5–6 tablespoons stock *or* water	⅓–½ cup stock *or* water
2 teaspoons tomato purée	2 teaspoons tomato purée	2 teaspoons tomato paste
8 oz. cooked buttered rice *or* noodles	225 g. cooked buttered rice *or* noodles	1½ cups cooked buttered rice *or* noodles

Discard any tissues or discoloured parts from livers. Cut each liver into 3 and toss in the seasoned flour. Cut gammon into dice. Melt the butter in a sauté pan, fry the gammon for 1 minute, add the livers and cook, stirring or tossing frequently until the livers change colour, about 2 minutes.

Stir in wine, stock and tomato purée and simmer very gently for 5 minutes. Serve livers on a bed of hot cooked buttered rice or ribbon noodles.

Pigeons with peas and celery

Cooking time: 1½ hours
Serves: 3

IMPERIAL	METRIC	AMERICAN
1 tablespoon oil	1 tablespoon oil	1 tablespoon oil
1 oz. butter	25 g. butter	2 tablespoons butter
4 oz. onion, chopped	100 g. onion, chopped	1 medium onion, chopped
2 oz. bacon	50 g. bacon	2 slices bacon
3 pigeons, prepared for cooking	3 pigeons, prepared for cooking	3 pigeons, prepared for cooking
¼ pint dry white wine	1½ dl. dry white wine	⅔ cup dry white wine
¼ pint chicken stock	1½ dl. chicken stock	⅔ cup chicken stock
salt and pepper	salt and pepper	salt and pepper
1 lb. shelled green peas, frozen *or* fresh	450 g. shelled green peas, frozen *or* fresh	3 cups shelled green peas, frozen *or* fresh
2 sticks celery, chopped	2 sticks celery, chopped	2 stalks celery, chopped

In a large heatproof casserole warm the oil and butter and over a low heat, fry the onion until golden, about 5 minutes. Add the bacon cut in strips and the pigeons; cook gently, turning the birds now and then, until browned all over. Add wine and bubble briskly for 2 minutes, then add stock and seasoning to taste. Cover closely and simmer gently for about 1¼ hours. Add the peas and celery and cook a further 15 to 20 minutes or until tender. Serve in the casserole. *Note.* Cooking time is for mature pigeons; if *known* to be young birds 1 hour will be long enough.

Breast of turkey in Marsala

Cooking time: 15–20 minutes
Serves: 4

IMPERIAL	METRIC	AMERICAN
1 lb. thinly sliced raw turkey breast meat	450 g. thinly sliced raw turkey breast meat	1 lb. thinly sliced raw turkey breast meat
½ lemon	½ lemon	½ lemon
little seasoned flour	little seasoned flour	little seasoned flour
2–3 oz. butter	50–75 g. butter	4–6 tablespoons butter
4 tablespoons Marsala	4 tablespoons Marsala	⅓ cup Marsala
4 tablespoons grated Parmesan	4 tablespoons grated Parmesan	⅓ cup grated Parmesan
4 tablespoons chicken stock	4 tablespoons chicken stock	⅓ cup chicken stock

A delicious Italian way of cooking turkey or chicken breast. Cut the turkey into convenient size pieces for serving and flatten with a knife. Rub over with the cut lemon, then coat with seasoned flour. Melt the butter in a large frying pan and, over gentle heat, fry the breasts for 10 minutes, turning until golden on both sides.

Pour over Marsala and allow to bubble for a minute or so. Sprinkle each fillet thickly with Parmesan and moisten with chicken stock. Cover pan and cook *gently* for another 5 to 10 minutes, until turkey is tender and the cheese melted. Serve with pan juices poured over. Braised chicory or celery, and new potatoes, are good vegetables to serve with this.

Roast duck Italian style

Cooking time: 2 hours
Temperature: 325°F., 170°C.,
  Gas Mark 3
Serves: 4

IMPERIAL	METRIC	AMERICAN
4-lb. duck	1¾-kg. duck	4-lb. duck
salt and ground black pepper	salt and ground black pepper	salt and ground black pepper
6 fresh sage leaves	6 fresh sage leaves	6 fresh sage leaves
1 small onion	1 small onion	1 small onion
2 tablespoons Marsala	2 tablespoons Marsala	3 tablespoons Marsala
1 tablespoon brandy	1 tablespoon brandy	1 tablespoon brandy
¼ pint stock *or* water	1½ dl. stock *or* water	⅔ cup stock *or* water
1 teaspoon lemon juice	1 teaspoon lemon juice	1 teaspoon lemon juice

This is a very suitable way of cooking frozen duck. Remove giblets and wash and dry duck. Sprinkle the bird inside and out with salt and pepper. Insert 4 sage leaves and the peeled onion into body cavity. Rub outside with crushed sage leaves and prick well to release fat. Place duck breast down in roasting tin with the giblets around. Cook in centre of the oven for 30 minutes. Then turn breast up and pour over the Marsala and brandy. Continue cooking, basting with the pan juices from time to time, for another 1½ hours, increasing the oven heat to 375°F., 190°C., Gas Mark 5, for the last 30 minutes to crisp the skin.

Dish the bird. Skim off fat from the roasting tin, add the stock and the lemon juice and bring to the boil. Strain into a gravy boat. Serve with roast potatoes, braised celery and green peas or beans.

Roast chicken with tomato and mushroom

Cooking time: 1½ hours
Temperature: 375°F., 190°C.,
  Gas Mark 5
Serves: 4–6

IMPERIAL	METRIC	AMERICAN
3-lb. roasting chicken, oven-ready	1½-kg. roasting chicken, oven-ready	3-lb. roasting chicken, oven-ready
1½ oz. butter	40 g. butter	3 tablespoons butter
salt and pepper	salt and pepper	salt and pepper
sprig of tarragon, if available	sprig of tarragon, if available	sprig of tarragon, if available
¼ pint chicken stock	1½ dl. chicken stock	⅔ cup chicken stock
¼ pint dry white wine	1½ dl. dry white wine	⅔ cup dry white wine
1 large onion, sliced	1 large onion, sliced	1 large onion, sliced
4 oz. button mushrooms	100 g. button mushrooms	1 cup button mushrooms
1 lb. ripe tomatoes, peeled and quartered	450 g. ripe tomatoes, peeled and quartered	1 lb. ripe tomatoes, peeled and quartered
1½ tablespoons flour	1½ tablespoons flour	2 tablespoons flour
1 oz. softened butter	25 g. softened butter	2 tablespoons softened butter
creamed potatoes (optional)	creamed potatoes (optional)	mashed potatoes (optional)
paprika (optional)	paprika (optional)	paprika (optional)
fresh watercress	fresh watercress	fresh watercress

Remove bag of giblets from chicken and put neck, gizzard, half the butter, some salt and pepper, and the tarragon, inside the bird. Smear rest of butter over breast and legs. Place chicken in roasting tin, covering breast lightly with greaseproof paper. Pour round the stock and wine. Roast in centre of preheated oven for 1 hour 20 minutes, basting occasionally.

When cooked, dish chicken and keep warm. Skim 2 tablespoons of fat from roasting tin, put into a pan and in it gently cook the onion until soft, about 5 minutes. Add chopped chicken liver and mushrooms and cook for another few minutes. Add rest of the juices from the pan and half the quartered tomatoes. Blend the flour and butter to a paste, and add little by little to the gravy, beating in smoothly. Bring the sauce to the boil and simmer for several minutes to thicken it. Season to taste, add remaining tomatoes and heat without stirring. Arrange round chicken. If liked, pipe swirls of creamed potato at intervals around dish, and sprinkle with paprika. Garnish with watercress.

Quick cooking meat dishes

You will remember that table wine used in cooking needs to be *cooked*. This is to drive off the alcohol, leaving behind the essences of the wine to add their rich savour to the dish. But how does one manage this in recipes which are cooked in ten minutes? The French, who have taught us so much about good cooking, have the answer – you simply reduce the wine by very fast boiling to about half its original quantity. This process is very much quicker if you use a *wide* pan. And of course the meat must first be removed so that it is not toughened or overcooked by the process. This basic technique gives us the beautifully simple recipes in this chapter. Steaks

cooked quickly in butter with the flavoursome wine sauce prepared in the same pan, and escalopes of veal in Marsala or cream sauce. For less grand occasions, exactly the same principle can be used for minced beef cakes, 'Bifteck haché à la lyonnaise' for example (see below).

For dishes where the wine is reduced by rapid boiling the flavour of the wine is all important and 'the better the wine the better the dish' is undoubtedly true. Ideally use a wine with good body such as a sound French Mâcon or Burgundy. Only a small amount is needed, so it may be quite possible to take a little from the bottle to be served with the meal.

Beefsteak with wine sauce

(illustrated on page 31)
Cooking time: 10 minutes
Serves: 4

IMPERIAL	METRIC	AMERICAN
4 rump *or* entrecôte steaks, $\frac{3}{4}$–1 inch thick	4 rump *or* entrecôte steaks, 2–2·5 cm. thick	4 sirloin *or* rib steaks, $\frac{3}{4}$–1 inch thick
2 oz. butter	50 g. butter	$\frac{1}{4}$ cup butter
1 tablespoon olive oil	1 tablespoon olive oil	1 tablespoon olive oil
salt and ground black pepper	salt and ground black pepper	salt and ground black pepper
$\frac{1}{4}$ pint red wine	$1\frac{1}{2}$ dl. red wine	$\frac{2}{3}$ cup red wine

Trim steaks and pat dry. Heat half the butter and the oil in a heavy pan and fry steaks over medium heat for 3 to 4 minutes each side. When small beads of red juice begin to ooze from the surface the steak is cooked medium rare (à point). Remove steaks, season and keep warm. Pour off any surplus or burnt fat. Add wine to pan and boil furiously, scraping up

coagulated juices with a wooden spoon, until reduced to about 4 tablespoons. Off the heat, stir in the remaining butter which will slightly thicken the sauce. Pour sauce over steaks and serve with sautéed mushrooms, tomatoes, watercress and a pat of parsley butter, if liked.

Bifteck haché à la lyonnaise

Cooking time: 10 minutes
Serves: 4

IMPERIAL	METRIC	AMERICAN
2 oz. chopped onion	50 g. chopped onion	$\frac{1}{3}$ cup chopped onion
2 tablespoons olive oil	2 tablespoons olive oil	3 tablespoons olive oil
1 lb. lean minced beef	450 g. lean minced beef	1 lb. lean ground beef
salt and ground black pepper	salt and ground black pepper	salt and ground black pepper
1 egg	1 egg	1 egg
little flour	little flour	little flour
$\frac{1}{4}$ pint red *or* white wine	$1\frac{1}{2}$ dl. red *or* white wine	$\frac{2}{3}$ cup red *or* white wine
1 oz. softened butter	25 g. softened butter	2 tablespoons softened butter

Fry the onions *slowly* in 1 tablespoon olive oil until soft but not browned, about 10 minutes. Put into a mixing bowl and add the beef, seasoning and egg; mix very thoroughly. Form into 4 round cakes about $\frac{3}{4}$ inch thick. Cover and keep in refrigerator until ready to cook, then coat lightly with flour. Heat remaining

oil in a heavy frying pan and when hot fry the cakes for 3 to 4 minutes each side. Dish and keep hot. Add the wine to the pan and boil rapidly, scraping up coagulated juices, until well reduced and syrupy. Off the heat stir in the butter and spoon the sauce over the meat.

Steaks with shallot and butter sauce

Cooking time: 10 minutes
Serves: 4

IMPERIAL	METRIC	AMERICAN
4 rump or fillet steaks, ¾ inch thick	4 rump or fillet steaks, 2 cm. thick	4 sirloin or tenderloin steaks, ¾ inch thick
3 oz. butter	75 g. butter	6 tablespoons butter
1 tablespoon vegetable oil	1 tablespoon vegetable oil	1 tablespoon vegetable oil
salt and ground black pepper	salt and ground black pepper	salt and ground black pepper
2 oz. finely chopped shallot or spring onion	50 g. finely chopped shallot or spring onion	⅓ cup finely chopped shallot or scallion
¼ pint dry white wine	1½ dl. dry white wine	⅔ cup dry white wine
1½ tablespoons chopped fresh parsley	1½ tablespoons chopped fresh parsley	2 tablespoons chopped fresh parsley
sprigs of watercress	sprigs of watercress	sprigs of watercress
miniature potato chips	miniature potato chips	thin French fries

Beat steaks to flatten slightly, and wipe dry. Heat 1 oz. butter and the oil in a heavy pan and when hot fry steaks fairly briskly for 3 to 4 minutes each side. When small beads of red juice begin to ooze from the surface the steak is cooked to the medium rare stage. Season steaks and transfer to hot serving dish.

Add ½ oz. butter and the shallots or spring onion to the frying pan and cook *gently* for 2 minutes (if you have to substitute onion cook for 5 minutes). Add wine, stir and scrape meat juices from bottom of pan, then bubble briskly until well reduced and almost syrupy. Off the heat add remaining butter in walnut size pieces stirring all the time – this will enrich and thicken the sauce. Check seasoning, add the parsley, and spoon sauce over steaks. Garnish with watercress and miniature chips.

French shepherds' pie

Cooking time: 20–25 minutes
Serves: 4

IMPERIAL	METRIC	AMERICAN
1 oz. dripping or lard	25 g. dripping or lard	2 tablespoons drippings or lard
1 onion, finely chopped	1 onion, finely chopped	1 onion, finely chopped
1 garlic clove, crushed	1 garlic clove, crushed	1 garlic clove, crushed
1 tablespoon flour	1 tablespoon flour	1 tablespoon flour
4 tablespoons white or red wine	4 tablespoons white or red wine	⅓ cup white or red wine
4 tablespoons stock or water	4 tablespoons stock or water	⅓ cup stock or water
2 ripe tomatoes, skinned and chopped, or 1 teaspoon tomato purée	2 ripe tomatoes, skinned and chopped, or 1 teaspoon tomato purée	2 ripe tomatoes, skinned and chopped, or 1 teaspoon tomato paste
1 lb. minced cooked meat	450 g. minced cooked meat	1 lb. ground cooked meat
1 tablespoon chopped parsley	1 tablespoon chopped parsley	1 tablespoon chopped parsley
salt and pepper	salt and pepper	salt and pepper
1½ lb. hot creamy mashed potato	700 g. hot creamy mashed potato	3 cups hot creamy mashed potato

Heat the fat in a saucepan and fry the onion gently until soft. Add the garlic and flour and stir and cook for a minute. Stir in the wine and stock, bring to the boil and simmer for 5 minutes. Off the heat, stir in the tomatoes or tomato purée, meat, parsley and season-ing to taste. Spread half the potato in the bottom of a shallow heatproof gratin dish, cover with meat mixture and top with remaining potato. Decorate, using a fork, and put under a hot grill to brown the surface.

Liver in Basque style

Cooking time: about 20 minutes
Serves: 4

IMPERIAL	METRIC	AMERICAN
2 aubergines	2 aubergines	2 eggplants
salt	salt	salt
4–5 tablespoons olive oil	4–5 tablespoons olive oil	about $\frac{1}{3}$ cup olive oil
2 medium onions, sliced	2 medium onions, sliced	2 medium onions, sliced
1 lb. lamb liver, sliced	450 g. lamb liver, sliced	1 lb. lamb liver, sliced
little seasoned flour	little seasoned flour	little seasoned flour
1 oz. butter	25 g. butter	2 tablespoons butter
1 garlic clove, crushed	1 garlic clove, crushed	1 garlic clove, crushed
1 lb. ripe tomatoes, skinned and quartered	450 g. ripe tomatoes, skinned and quartered	1 lb. ripe tomatoes, skinned and quartered
3 tablespoons medium dry white *or* rosé wine	3 tablespoons medium dry white *or* rosé wine	$\frac{1}{4}$ cup medium dry white *or* rosé wine

Cut the aubergines into $\frac{1}{4}$-inch thick slices, sprinkle with salt, and leave in a colander to drain for 1 hour. Heat 3 tablespoons of oil in a large frying pan and when hot fry the drained and dried aubergine slices until brown on both sides. Remove and keep hot. If necessary add a little more oil to the pan and fry the onions until golden; then remove and keep hot. Sprinkle the liver slices with seasoned flour and fry quickly in the same pan for 2 minutes each side.

Meanwhile, in another pan melt the butter, add the garlic and tomatoes, stir, and leave to heat through gently. Arrange alternate slices of liver and aubergine around a hot serving dish. Swill the frying pan with the wine, stir and boil rapidly until syrupy then pour over the liver. Pile the tomatoes and fried onions in the centre of the dish, and serve very hot.

Veal escalopes with cream sauce

Cooking time: 15 minutes
Serves: 4

IMPERIAL	METRIC	AMERICAN
4 thin veal escalopes, about 3–4 oz. each	4 thin veal escalopes, about 75–100 g. each	4 thin veal escalopes, about 3–4 oz. each
salt and pepper	salt and pepper	salt and pepper
little lemon juice	little lemon juice	little lemon juice
about 2 oz. butter	about 50 g. butter	about $\frac{1}{4}$ cup butter
4 tablespoons dry white vermouth, white wine *or* Madeira	4 tablespoons dry white vermouth, white wine *or* Madeira	$\frac{1}{3}$ cup dry white vermouth, white wine *or* Madeira
$\frac{1}{4}$ pint double cream	$1\frac{1}{2}$ dl. double cream	$\frac{2}{3}$ cup whipping cream
few fresh tarragon leaves	few fresh tarragon leaves	few fresh tarragon leaves
sautéed button mushrooms	sautéed button mushrooms	sautéed button mushrooms

Season escalopes with salt, pepper and lemon juice. Heat $1\frac{1}{2}$ oz. butter in a large frying pan and fry escalopes two at a time, for 3 to 4 minutes each side. Remove and keep hot. Add wine to pan, stir and bubble briskly until syrupy. Add the cream and tarragon leaves, and stir gently until sauce thickens very slightly. Replace meat and heat gently for 4 to 5 minutes. Dish escalopes and spoon the thickened sauce over. Garnish with the mushrooms.

Intoxicated pork chops

(*illustrated on page 51*)
Cooking time: 35 minutes
Serves: 4

IMPERIAL	METRIC	AMERICAN
4 thick lean pork chops	4 thick lean pork chops	4 thick lean pork chops
salt and pepper	salt and pepper	salt and pepper
3 tablespoons olive oil	3 tablespoons olive oil	$\frac{1}{4}$ cup olive oil
2 garlic cloves, crushed	2 garlic cloves, crushed	2 garlic cloves, crushed
2 tablespoons chopped parsley	2 tablespoons chopped parsley	3 tablespoons chopped parsley
6 tablespoons rosé *or* light red wine	6 tablespoons rosé *or* light red wine	$\frac{1}{2}$ cup rosé *or* light red wine
sprig parsley	sprig parsley	sprig parsley

A gay Italian recipe. Season the chops with salt and pepper. Heat the oil, garlic and parsley in a wide saucepan with lid and when hot put in the chops. Fry over *gentle* heat until golden on both sides, about 15 minutes. Add the wine, cover the pan closely and cook gently until the meat has absorbed most of the wine, about 20 minutes.

Pour the remaining pan juices over the chops and garnish with parsley.

If liked, serve with grilled halved tomatoes, sauteed button onions and roast potatoes.

Savoy pork chops

Cooking time: about 30 minutes
Serves: 4

IMPERIAL	METRIC	AMERICAN
1 tablespoon vegetable oil	1 tablespoon vegetable oil	1 tablespoon vegetable oil
4 pork chops*	4 pork chops*	4 pork chops*
2 large cooking apples	2 large cooking apples	2 large cooking apples
2 oz. seedless raisins	50 g. seedless raisins	⅓ cup seedless raisins
finely grated rind 1 orange	finely grated rind 1 orange	finely grated rind 1 orange
⅓ pint apple (dry) wine	2 dl. apple (dry) wine	scant 1 cup apple (dry) wine
salt and pepper	salt and pepper	salt and pepper
fried apple rings	fried apple rings	fried apple rings

Heat the oil in a large shallow pan and fry the chops steadily until golden both sides, about 5 minutes. Lower the heat and add the peeled, cored and sliced apples, raisins, orange rind and wine, with seasoning to taste. Cover tightly and simmer *gently* for 25 to 30 minutes, turning the chops at half time. Lift out the chops, stir the apples so that they form an apple sauce with the wine and raisins. Serve the chops on top of the apple sauce, garnished with fried apple rings.

*Thick slices of lean belly pork are good cooked this way too, and cheaper.

Roman style veal and ham

Cooking time: 10–15 minutes
Serves: 4

IMPERIAL	METRIC	AMERICAN
8 thin slices veal fillet	8 thin slices veal fillet	8 thin slices veal cutlet
ground black pepper	ground black pepper	ground black pepper
4 oz. raw ham, *thinly* sliced	100 g. raw ham, *thinly* sliced	¼ lb. raw ham, *thinly* sliced
8 fresh sage leaves	8 fresh sage leaves	8 fresh sage leaves
about 2 oz. butter	about 50 g. butter	about ¼ cup butter
about 4 tablespoons dry white wine	about 4 tablespoons dry white wine	about ⅓ cup dry white wine

Beat the slices of veal until very thin and about 4 inches square, and season with pepper. Cut the ham into similar size pieces and place flat on top of the veal with one sage leaf sandwiched between or on top. Secure with a toothpick.

Heat a little butter in a frying pan and fry the meat (half at a time if necessary) over moderate heat until golden on both sides. Add the wine, cover, reduce the heat and simmer for 10 to 15 minutes or until tender. Remove toothpicks and arrange ham-side up on a serving dish. Add a nut of butter to the pan juices, stir well and pour over the meat.

Noisette of pork with prunes

Cooking time: 35–40 minutes
Serves: 4

IMPERIAL	METRIC	AMERICAN
12 large prunes	12 large prunes	12 large prunes
$\frac{2}{3}$ pint dry white wine	4 dl. dry white wine	$1\frac{3}{4}$ cups dry white wine
1–1$\frac{1}{4}$ lb. boneless pork fillet	450–600 g. boneless pork fillet	1–1$\frac{1}{4}$ lb. boneless pork tenderloin
seasoned flour	seasoned flour	seasoned flour
1–2 oz. butter	25–50 g. butter	2–4 tablespoons butter
1 tablespoon vegetable oil	1 tablespoon vegetable oil	1 tablespoon vegetable oil
1 tablespoon redcurrant jelly	1 tablespoon redcurrant jelly	1 tablespoon red currant jelly
4 fl. oz. double cream	1 dl. double cream	$\frac{1}{2}$ cup whipping cream

Soak prunes overnight in $\frac{1}{2}$ pint of the wine. Next day simmer until tender, about 30 minutes. Trim any fat or skin from pork fillet, and holding knife in slanting position cut across into 2-inch slices. Flatten slightly with a damp rolling pin, then coat with seasoned flour. Heat butter and oil in a sauté pan and fry meat gently for 5 minutes each side; add remaining wine, cover and simmer until tender, about 20 minutes. Arrange meat down centre of serving dish and keep hot. Strain wine from prunes into sauté pan, stir and scrape juices from bottom of pan, then boil fast until reduced to $\frac{1}{3}$ pint. Add the jelly and when dissolved stir in the cream. Boil until thick then pour over meat, and arrange warm prunes on either side.

Sauté kidneys with Madeira

Cooking time: 10–12 minutes
Serves: 4

IMPERIAL	METRIC	AMERICAN
3 veal *or* 8 lamb kidneys	3 veal *or* 8 lamb kidneys	3 veal *or* 8 lamb kidneys
1 oz. butter	25 g. butter	2 tablespoons butter
1 tablespoon flour	1 tablespoon flour	1 tablespoon flour
$\frac{1}{4}$ pint stock	1$\frac{1}{2}$ dl. stock	$\frac{2}{3}$ cup stock
3 tablespoons Madeira	3 tablespoons Madeira	$\frac{1}{4}$ cup Madeira
salt and pepper	salt and pepper	salt and pepper
1 teaspoon lemon juice	1 teaspoon lemon juice	1 teaspoon lemon juice
toast triangles	toast triangles	toast triangles
1 tablespoon chopped parsley	1 tablespoon chopped parsley	1 tablespoon chopped parsley

Skin kidneys and cut into slices. Heat butter in a frying pan and fry kidneys fairly briskly for 3 to 4 minutes, turning to brown both sides. Remove, cover and keep warm. Sprinkle flour into pan, stir and cook for 1 to 2 minutes until brown. Stir in the stock and Madeira and seasoning to taste; simmer for 5 minutes. Replace kidneys and any juices; add lemon juice and heat without boiling for several minutes. Serve with toast triangles and parsley garnish.

Long cooking meat dishes

This chapter covers meat dishes needing longer than an hour to cook. Some require much longer.

The main point in adding wine to meat dishes is simply that it enriches the flavour as nothing else can. This is true of high quality meat, say a whole fillet of beef basted with wine during roasting, and even more true of the cheaper cuts which can be transformed by a long and gentle simmering with wine, herbs and vegetables. During a long slow cook the wine also helps to tenderise the meat fibres.

What wine should you use? Obviously one would not normally use an expensive vintage wine for cooking, but at the same time it must be emphasised that a too cheap 'thin' wine will produce nothing but a disappointing result. Aim for a sound, dryish and full flavoured wine, red or white, that you would enjoy drinking. It is the essential flavour of the wine that remains to enrich the dish after the alcohol has gone.

Marinating in wine

Nowadays the purpose of marinating meat is to impart flavour and to help tenderise the fibres. So, generally speaking the meats to benefit most are braising and stewing cuts. Basically this type of marinade consists of red or white wine, olive oil, seasonings, herbs and thickly sliced onions and carrots. The addition of wine vinegar, garlic or brandy will strengthen the marinade, and juniper berries (or a tablespoon or two of gin) and coriander seeds help to impart a gamy flavour. Sliced vegetables go in the bottom of a large china bowl with the well seasoned meat on top, the wine, oil and vinegar are then poured over and the meat topped with herbs and more vegetables. The meat must be turned or stirred frequently so that all parts are impregnated. The marinating can last from a few hours to several days depending on the toughness of the meat or degree of the flavour required. Marinades that are to last several days are first cooked to ensure that the vegetables will not turn sour. If the meat is to be roasted it must of course be carefully dried after removal from the marinade. The strained marinade is then reduced and used for the sauce or gravy.

Wine in casseroles and stews

If you replace half the liquid with wine in any standard casserole or stew recipe, the flavour will be much more interesting. Country and home-made wines come into their own here, and cider too. In many cases the proportion can be increased, especially if you like a strong flavour, but you *can* overdo it.

Basting with wine

Meat, and poultry too, can be basted with wine during cooking, and an excellent gravy made from the wine and drippings in the roast tin. You can use wine straight from the bottle, or better still first concentrate it by rapid boiling in an open pan until well reduced. About $\frac{1}{4}$ pint concentrated to 4–5 tablespoons is ample for a family roast. Roast veal in particular benefits from this treatment. Even a few tablespoonfuls of white wine poured over the roast half an hour before dishing up will improve the gravy.

Beef with olives

Cooking time: $2\frac{1}{2}$–3 hours
Temperature: 300°F., 150°C.,
   Gas Mark 2
Serves: 4

IMPERIAL	METRIC	AMERICAN
$1\frac{1}{2}$ lb. chuck steak	700 g. chuck steak	$1\frac{1}{2}$ lb. chuck steak
$\frac{3}{4}$ oz. cornflour	20 g. cornflour	$2\frac{1}{2}$ tablespoons cornstarch
3 tablespoons oil	3 tablespoons oil	$\frac{1}{4}$ cup vegetable oil
4–8 button onions	4–8 button onions	4–8 tiny onions
3 carrots, sliced	3 carrots, sliced	3 carrots, sliced
1–2 garlic cloves	1–2 garlic cloves	1–2 garlic cloves
4 oz. mushrooms	100 g. mushrooms	1 cup sliced mushrooms
$\frac{1}{4}$ pint robust red wine	$1\frac{1}{2}$ dl. robust red wine	$\frac{2}{3}$ cup robust red wine
$\frac{1}{2}$ pint meat stock	3 dl. meat stock	$1\frac{1}{4}$ cups meat stock
few black olives	few black olives	few ripe olives

Cut the meat into 1-inch cubes and coat with the cornflour to which a little salt and pepper has been added. Heat the oil in a frying pan and fry the meat for several minutes, turning to brown lightly on all sides. Remove meat and put into a casserole.

Put the onions, carrots and garlic into the frying pan with any remaining cornflour, and stir around for a few minutes; add to the casserole with the sliced mushrooms. Pour the wine into the frying pan, stir around, then bubble briskly for several minutes. Add the stock, and bring to the boil, and pour over the meat in the casserole. Cover tightly and cook in the centre of the oven for at least 2 hours. Half an hour before serving add the well washed olives. Season.

Leg of lamb tasting like venison

Cooking time: 2–2½ hours
Temperature: 350°F., 180°C.,
  Gas Mark 4
Serves: 10–12

IMPERIAL	METRIC	AMERICAN
4–5-lb. leg of lean mutton *or* lamb	2–2¼-kg. leg of lean mutton *or* lamb	4–5-lb. leg of lean mutton *or* lamb
4 tablespoons olive oil	4 tablespoons olive oil	⅓ cup olive oil
1 onion, sliced	1 onion, sliced	1 onion, sliced
1 carrot, sliced	1 carrot, sliced	1 carrot, sliced
1 stick celery, sliced	1 stick celery, sliced	1 stalk celery, sliced
1 garlic clove, halved	1 garlic clove, halved	1 garlic clove, halved
1¼ pints robust red wine	¾ litre robust red wine	3 cups robust red wine
¼ pint red wine vinegar	1½ dl. red wine vinegar	⅔ cup red wine vinegar
2 teaspoons salt	2 teaspoons salt	2 teaspoons salt
½ teaspoon black peppercorns	½ teaspoon black peppercorns	½ teaspoon black peppercorns
1 bay leaf	1 bay leaf	1 bay leaf
sprig each rosemary, thyme and parsley	sprig each rosemary, thyme and parsley	sprig each rosemary, thyme and parsley
4 crushed juniper berries	4 crushed juniper berries	4 crushed juniper berries
sauce	*sauce*	*sauce*
¼ pint strained marinade	1½ dl. strained marinade	⅔ cup strained marinade
¾ pint stock *or* water	4½ dl. stock *or* water	2 cups stock *or* water
2 tablespoons flour	2 tablespoons flour	3 tablespoons flour
1 tablespoon redcurrant jelly	1 tablespoon redcurrant jelly	1 tablespoon red currant jelly
salt and pepper	salt and pepper	salt and pepper

If you like a gamy flavour this is an interesting and tasty way of dealing with mature lamb or mutton. Skin the leg of lamb and remove all surplus fat. To make the marinade, heat the oil and fry the vegetables slowly in a covered saucepan for 5 minutes, without colouring. Add the wine, vinegar, seasonings, spices and herbs. Simmer gently for 15 minutes then allow to cool completely. Place the leg in a deep china, glass or enamelled basin and pour the cold marinade over. Turn and baste several times a day, for 4 to 5 days at room temperature, or 6 to 7 days in a refrigerator or a winter larder. To cook, drain the leg well (reserving the marinade), then dry thoroughly with kitchen paper. Roast in the usual way allowing 30 minutes per lb.

An hour before dishing up, start simmering the strained marinade and stock or water in a covered pan. After dishing the joint, strain off all but 2 tablespoons of fat from roasting tin, stir in flour and cook, stirring, for 2 minutes until lightly browned. Stir in marinade and stock and the redcurrant jelly. Boil up and simmer for 5 minutes. Check seasoning and serve with the joint. Vegetables that go well with this dish are braised celery or chicory, or red cabbage with chestnuts. Any leftovers are excellent cold, with an orange and watercress salad.

Boeuf à la bourguignonne

Cooking time: 2½–3 hours
Serves: 4

IMPERIAL	METRIC	AMERICAN
2 thick slices salt belly pork	2 thick slices salt belly pork	2 thick slices salt pork
1 oz. dripping *or* lard	25 g. dripping *or* lard	2 tablespoons drippings *or* lard
12 peeled button onions	12 peeled button onions	12 peeled tiny onions
4 oz. chopped onions	100 g. chopped onions	1 medium onion, chopped
1½ lb. blade *or* chuck steak, in 1-inch cubes	700 g. blade *or* chuck steak, in 2·5-cm. cubes	1½ lb. chuck steak *or* other lean beef, in 1-inch cubes
2 tablespoons flour	2 tablespoons flour	3 tablespoons flour
¼ pint robust red wine	1½ dl. robust red wine	⅔ cup robust red wine
½ pint beef stock *or* water with stock cube	3 dl. beef stock *or* water with stock cube	1¼ cups beef stock *or* water with bouillon cube
1 tablespoon tomato purée	1 tablespoon tomato purée	1 tablespoon tomato paste
1 garlic clove, crushed	1 garlic clove, crushed	1 garlic clove, crushed
bouquet of bay leaf, thyme and parsley, tied	bouquet of bay leaf, thyme and parsley, tied	bouquet of bay leaf, thyme and parsley, tied
salt and ground black pepper	salt and ground black pepper	salt and ground black pepper
4 oz. button mushrooms, sautéed in butter	100 g. button mushrooms, sautéed in butter	1 cup button mushrooms, sautéed in butter

This is a typical French beef and wine casserole, and worth making in double quantities as it reheats or freezes excellently. Cut pork into ¼-inch strips. Melt fat in a heatproof casserole and fry pork and button onions slowly, stirring frequently, until golden; remove onions and reserve. Add chopped onion and meat to casserole and fry briskly, stirring frequently, until browned. Sprinkle in the flour, stir and cook for a minute. Stir in wine, allow to bubble for a minute, then add stock, tomato purée, garlic, herbs and seasoning. When boiling, cover tightly and simmer *very gently* on top of cooker (if more convenient cook in a slow oven, 300°F., 150°C., Gas Mark 2) for at least 2 hours. Check seasoning, add button onions and mushrooms. Cover and cook for another 30 minutes. Serve from the casserole, with boiled potatoes tossed in butter and sprinkled with parsley. With this drink a full bodied red wine.

Braised rump steak with wine and tomatoes

Cooking time: about 2 hours
Temperature: 300°F., 150°C., Gas Mark 2
Serves: 4

IMPERIAL	METRIC	AMERICAN
1½-lb. slice rump steak, 1½ inches thick	700-g. slice rump steak, 3·5 cm. thick	1½-lb. slice round steak, 1½ inches thick
1 cut garlic clove	1 cut garlic clove	1 cut garlic clove
2 tablespoons olive oil	2 tablespoons olive oil	3 tablespoons olive oil
salt and ground black pepper	salt and ground black pepper	salt and ground black pepper
1 large onion	1 large onion	1 large onion
2 medium carrots	2 medium carrots	2 medium carrots
4 tablespoons dry white wine	4 tablespoons dry white wine	⅓ cup dry white wine
4 tablespoons Madeira *or* sherry	4 tablespoons Madeira *or* sherry	⅓ cup Madeira *or* sherry
2 tablespoons brandy	2 tablespoons brandy	3 tablespoons brandy
4 ripe tomatoes	4 ripe tomatoes	4 ripe tomatoes

Dry the meat with kitchen paper, and rub each side with the cut clove of garlic. Heat the oil in a flameproof casserole and quickly brown the steak on each side. Remove and season. Fry the sliced onion and carrots in the same oil until beginning to colour; then replace the steak on top. Add the wine, Madeira or brandy and allow to simmer for 1 to 2 minutes. Peel and quarter the tomatoes, scatter over the meat and season lightly.

Cover the casserole tightly with foil and the lid. Cook in centre of oven for about 2 hours. If possible keep the dish covered until the moment of serving so that everyone can enjoy the wonderful aroma when the lid is lifted. Serve with a light potato purée.

Paupiettes of beef

Cooking time: 1½–2 hours
Temperature: 325°F., 170°C.,
 Gas Mark 3
Serves 4

IMPERIAL	METRIC	AMERICAN
4 large thin slices buttock steak	4 large thin slices buttock steak	4 large thin slices top round steak
4 thin rashers streaky bacon, de-rinded	4 thin rashers streaky bacon, de-rinded	4 slices bacon
2 teaspoons chopped fresh *or* ½ teaspoon dried marjoram	2 teaspoons chopped fresh *or* ½ teaspoon dried marjoram	2 teaspoons chopped fresh *or* ½ teaspoon dried marjoram
ground black pepper	ground black pepper	ground black pepper
1 oz. lard	25 g. lard	2 tablespoons lard
1 large onion, thinly sliced	1 large onion, thinly sliced	1 large onion, thinly sliced
1 tablespoon flour	1 tablespoon flour	1 tablespoon flour
¼ pint red wine	1½ dl. red wine	⅔ cup red wine
¼ pint meat stock	1½ dl. meat stock	⅔ cup meat stock
boiled rice	boiled rice	boiled rice

Ask the butcher to beat the steaks as thin as possible. Lay a rasher of bacon on each, sprinkle with herbs and black pepper. Roll up and secure with a poultry skewer or cocktail stick.

Heat the lard in a flameproof casserole and fry the steak rolls fairly briskly until lightly browned all over; remove. Fry the onion *gently* until beginning to colour, then stir in the flour and cook for a minute.

Add the wine, allow to bubble briskly for several minutes, then add the stock and bring to the boil. Check the seasoning, replace the meat and cover the casserole closely. Cook in centre of preheated oven until tender, turning the rolls at half time. To serve, remove the skewers, and arrange the rolls on a bed of boiled rice with the onions on top and a little of the sauce poured over each.

Ossobuco alla milanese

Cooking time: 1¾ hours
Serves: 3–4

IMPERIAL	METRIC	AMERICAN
1 meaty veal knuckle	1 meaty veal knuckle	1 meaty veal shank or shin
little flour	little flour	little flour
3 tablespoons olive oil	3 tablespoons olive oil	¼ cup olive oil
1 small onion, sliced	1 small onion, sliced	1 small onion, sliced
1 small carrot, sliced	1 small carrot, sliced	1 small carrot, sliced
1 stick celery, sliced	1 stick celery, sliced	1 stalk celery, sliced
1 bay leaf	1 bay leaf	1 bay leaf
4 fl. oz. white wine	1 dl. white wine	½ cup white wine
14-oz. can tomatoes	400-g. can tomatoes	14-oz. can tomatoes
salt and ground black pepper	salt and ground black pepper	salt and ground black pepper
1 garlic clove, crushed	1 garlic clove, crushed	1 garlic clove, crushed
½ teaspoon finely grated lemon rind	½ teaspoon finely grated lemon rind	½ teaspoon finely grated lemon rind
2 tablespoons chopped parsley	2 tablespoons chopped parsley	3 tablespoons chopped parsley

Have the ossobuco cut from a hind quarter of veal, sawn across the shin in 2-inch slices so each piece includes the bone (and marrow) with a good portion of meat around it. Coat the meat with flour. Heat the oil in a large saucepan and fry the meat in a single layer until browned on both sides; remove carefully as the marrow must remain in the bone. Add vegetables and bay leaf to pan, fry over low heat for 5 minutes. Add the wine and cook until almost evaporated, then stir in the contents of the can of

tomatoes, and seasoning to taste. Bring to the boil, replace the ossobuco, cover tightly and simmer *gently* until tender, about 1½ hours.

Dish the ossobuco and keep hot. Pass the vegetables and gravy through a sieve, foodmill or electric blender to form a medium thick sauce; if necessary boil for a few minutes to reduce. Add the garlic, lemon rind and parsley and check the seasoning. Bring to the boil and pour over the meat. Ossobuco is traditionally served with a Milanese risotto.

Pork stewed with wine and tomatoes

Cooking time: 1¾ hours
Temperature: 300°F., 150°C.,
  Gas Mark 2
Serves: 4

IMPERIAL	METRIC	AMERICAN
1½ lb. boneless shoulder of pork	700 g. boneless shoulder of pork	1½ lb. boneless shoulder of pork
1 oz. lard	25 g. lard	2 tablespoons lard
2 onions, chopped	2 onions, chopped	2 onions, chopped
2 tablespoons flour	2 tablespoons flour	3 tablespoons flour
⅓ pint medium dry white wine	2 dl. medium dry white wine	scant 1 cup medium dry white wine
2 teaspoons sugar	2 teaspoons sugar	2 teaspoons sugar
½ bay leaf	½ bay leaf	½ bay leaf
salt and ground black pepper	salt and ground black pepper	salt and ground black pepper
8-oz. can tomatoes	225-g. can tomatoes	8-oz. can tomatoes

Cut meat into 1-inch cubes. Heat lard in ovenproof casserole, add meat, stir until brown, then remove. In the same fat fry onions until beginning to colour then stir in flour and cook for 1 minute. Add wine, sugar, bay leaf, salt and pepper and contents of can of tomatoes; bring to the boil. Replace the meat. Cover tightly with foil and lid and cook in centre of oven for 1½ hours. Serve with boiled rice.

Veal and tomato casserole

Cooking time: 1½ hours
Temperature: 300°F., 150°C.,
  Gas Mark 2
Serves: 4

IMPERIAL	METRIC	AMERICAN
1½ lb. stewing veal, without bone	700 g. stewing veal, without bone	1½ lb. veal stew meat, without bone
1 tablespoon olive oil	1 tablespoon olive oil	1 tablespoon olive oil
1 oz. butter	25 g. butter	2 tablespoons butter
4 oz. chopped onion	100 g. chopped onion	1 medium onion, chopped
1 tablespoon seasoned flour	1 tablespoon seasoned flour	1 tablespoon seasoned flour
¼ pint dry white wine	1½ dl. dry white wine	⅔ cup dry white wine
scant ¼ pint chicken stock	1 dl. chicken stock	½ cup chicken stock
8 oz. ripe tomatoes *or* 8-oz. can tomatoes	225 g. ripe tomatoes *or* 225-g. can tomatoes	½ lb. ripe tomatoes *or* 8-oz. can tomatoes
1 garlic clove, crushed	1 garlic clove, crushed	1 garlic clove, crushed
small strip orange rind	small strip orange rind	small strip orange rind
bay leaf and sprig thyme, tied	bay leaf and sprig thyme, tied	bay leaf and sprig thyme, tied
4 oz. button mushrooms, sliced	100 g. button mushrooms, sliced	1 cup sliced button mushrooms
little chopped parsley	little chopped parsley	little chopped parsley

Cut veal into 2-inch pieces. Heat oil and butter in a heatproof casserole and fry veal and onion, stirring frequently, until golden. Sprinkle the flour over, stir and cook for a minute, then stir in wine and stock and bring to the boil. Peel, quarter and de-seed tomatoes or drain canned tomatoes. Add to the casserole with the garlic, orange rind, bay leaf and thyme. Cover tightly, and cook in centre of oven for 1¼ hours. Stir in mushrooms, cover casserole and cook for another 15 minutes. Remove orange rind and herbs, check seasoning, and serve sprinkled with parsley.

Braised gammon with Marsala

Cooking time: $1\frac{1}{2}$ hours
Serves: 6

IMPERIAL	METRIC	AMERICAN
2 lb. middle cut lean gammon	1 kg. middle cut lean gammon	2 lb. ham, butt half
$\frac{1}{5}$–$\frac{1}{4}$ pint Marsala	1–$1\frac{1}{2}$ dl. Marsala	$\frac{1}{2}$–$\frac{2}{3}$ cup Marsala
3 tablespoons olive oil	3 tablespoons olive oil	scant $\frac{1}{4}$ cup olive oil
1 large onion, sliced	1 large onion, sliced	1 large onion, sliced
2 large carrots, sliced	2 large carrots, sliced	2 large carrots, sliced
2 sticks celery, sliced	2 sticks celery, sliced	2 stalks celery, sliced
2 sprigs of parsley	2 sprigs of parsley	2 sprigs of parsley
pepper	pepper	pepper
1 bay leaf	1 bay leaf	1 bay leaf
$\frac{1}{2}$ pint stock *or* water	3 dl. stock *or* water	$1\frac{1}{4}$ cups stock *or* water

Soak the gammon overnight in cold water. Drain and dry. Pour Marsala over gammon and leave for several hours, turning at intervals. When ready to cook, heat the olive oil in a thick saucepan, stir in the onion, carrots, celery and parsley, cover the pan and cook over very low heat for 5 minutes. Drain the gammon (reserving wine) and lay on top of vegetables, adding the bay leaf and stock. Cover pan tightly and braise over low heat for $1\frac{1}{4}$ to $1\frac{1}{2}$ hours.

When cooked, skin and slice the gammon and arrange in an ovenproof dish. Press the vegetables and stock through a strainer or pulverise in an electric blender, add the reserved wine and boil for several minutes; check seasoning and pour over gammon. Cover, and leave in a cool oven (so that gammon becomes impregnated with the delicious sauce) until ready to serve. A purée of spinach or sliced and buttered courgettes go well with this.

Note. Any remainders come to no harm reheated next day, covered, in a slow oven.

Stuffed lamb roll

Cooking time: $1\frac{3}{4}$ hours
Serves: 4–5

IMPERIAL	METRIC	AMERICAN
1 lean breast of lamb, boned	1 lean breast of lamb, boned	1 lean breast of lamb, boned
pepper	pepper	pepper
thin slice of gammon	thin slice of gammon	thin slice of ham
2–3 hard-boiled eggs	2–3 hard-boiled eggs	2–3 hard-cooked eggs
1 oz. butter	25 g. butter	2 tablespoons butter
1 tablespoon oil	1 tablespoon oil	1 tablespoon oil
$\frac{1}{4}$ pint white wine	$1\frac{1}{2}$ dl. white wine	$\frac{2}{3}$ cup white wine
sprig of thyme *or* sage leaf	sprig of thyme *or* sage leaf	sprig of thyme *or* sage leaf

Ask your butcher to cut you a wide breast of lamb and to bone it. Flatten out the meat. Sprinkle with pepper and lay the gammon slice on top. Arrange the eggs, end to end, across the centre. Roll up the meat to form a neat roll and tie securely with string.

Heat the butter and oil in a heavy saucepan and fry the meat until golden on all sides. Add the wine and herbs, cover pan closely, and simmer very gently for about $1\frac{1}{2}$ hours. Serve hot, cut in slices with the juices poured over, or cool in the liquid and serve cold with salad.

Intoxicated pork chops (see recipe on page 42)

Cold sweets

A large number of cold desserts demand, or are immeasurably improved by, the addition of wine or spirits. There are some intriguing ideas, such as the Scotch mist on page 57 flavoured with Drambuie and honey, or the liqueur-flavoured Cream cheese cups on page 53. We start the chapter with that treasure of British inventions – the 'syllabub'. They say the 'syllabub' was born when an absent-minded milkmaid milked the cow straight into a pail of beer or cider. The resulting froth must have been popular because the syllabub idea has been evolving ever since. Of those given here the Solid syllabub is the late eighteenth century version, and is exquisite.

Solid syllabub

Serves: 5–6

IMPERIAL	METRIC	AMERICAN
$\frac{1}{2}$ lemon	$\frac{1}{2}$ lemon	$\frac{1}{2}$ lemon
6 tablespoons medium *or* sweet white wine	6 tablespoons medium *or* sweet white wine	$\frac{1}{2}$ cup medium *or* sweet white wine ·
2 tablespoons brandy*	2 tablespoons brandy*	3 tablespoons brandy*
2–3 oz. sifted icing sugar	50–75 g. sifted icing sugar	$\frac{1}{2}$–$\frac{3}{4}$ cup sifted confectioners' sugar
$\frac{1}{2}$ pint double cream	3 dl. double cream	$1\frac{1}{4}$ cups heavy cream

The texture and flavour of this syllabub improves if made the day before it is served. Put the thinly pared rind, the strained juice, wine, brandy and sugar (the amount of sugar depends on the sweetness of the wine) into a large bowl. Leave for at least 3 hours, or overnight. Remove lemon rind. Add cream and whisk steadily until the mixture is thick enough to stand in soft peaks. Pile into small fluted or custard glasses and leave in a cool place for several hours before serving.

*Substitute extra wine for brandy if preferred.

Variation
Raisin syllabub
Soak 1 to 2 oz. seedless raisins in the lemon and wine mixture.

Separated syllabub

Serves: 5–6

IMPERIAL	METRIC	AMERICAN
2 egg whites	2 egg whites	2 egg whites
4 oz. castor sugar	100 g. castor sugar	1 cup granulated sugar
juice of $\frac{1}{2}$ lemon	juice of $\frac{1}{2}$ lemon	juice of $\frac{1}{2}$ lemon
$\frac{1}{4}$ pint sweet white wine	$1\frac{1}{2}$ dl. sweet white wine	$\frac{2}{3}$ cup sweet white wine
$\frac{1}{2}$ pint double cream	3 dl. double cream	$1\frac{1}{4}$ cups heavy cream
twists of thinly pared lemon rind	twists of thinly pared lemon rind	twists of thinly pared lemon rind

In this syllabub the mixture separates, giving a frothy foam on top and a lemony wine whey beneath. Make in the morning for the evening. Whisk the egg whites until stiff. Then fold in the sugar, lemon juice and wine. Lightly whip the cream until thick but not stiff, and fold into the egg white mixture. Spoon into tall slim glasses of about 6 fl. oz. capacity and leave to separate. Decorate with a twist of lemon peel, and serve with crisp savoy biscuits.

Zabaglione

Cooking time: about 7 minutes
Serves: 4

IMPERIAL	METRIC	AMERICAN
4 large egg yolks	4 large egg yolks	4 egg yolks
3 tablespoons castor sugar	3 tablespoons castor sugar	¼ cup granulated sugar
¼ pint Marsala and white wine mixed	1½ dl. Marsala and white wine mixed	⅔ cup Marsala and white wine mixed

Marsala varies in strength and sweetness so adjust the proportions of white wine to suit your own taste. If there is no white wine handy try 6 tablespoons Marsala and 2 of water.

Put the egg yolks and sugar into a large basin and whisk with a balloon whisk until pale and frothy. Stir in the Marsala and wine. Stand the basin over a saucepan of near boiling water and beat continu-ously until the mixture froths and becomes thick and mousse-like *throughout*, which it will in a matter of minutes. Immediately remove from the heat, pour into glasses and serve right away with sponge finger biscuits. If the zabaglione is cooked to the right stage it will not separate in the glasses, but take care not to let it overcook and curdle.

Variations *Cold zabaglione*
Make as above but as soon as thickened remove from heat. Whisk from time to time until cold then fold in ¼ pint whipped cream and 1 stiffly beaten egg white.
Zabaglione with Madeira or sherry
Substitute Madeira or sherry for Marsala.

Irish trifles

Serves: 4

IMPERIAL	METRIC	AMERICAN
4-oz. packet ratafia biscuits	100 g. ratafia biscuits	¼ lb. ratafias or small macaroons
4 tablespoons Irish whiskey	4 tablespoons Irish whiskey	⅓ cup Irish whiskey
15-oz. can apricot halves	425-g. can apricot halves	15-oz. can apricot halves
2 eggs	2 eggs	2 eggs
2 tablespoons castor sugar	2 tablespoons castor sugar	3 tablespoons granulated sugar
½ pint milk	3 dl. milk	1¼ cups milk
¼ pint double cream	1½ dl. double cream	⅔ cup whipping cream
flaked almonds, toasted	flaked almonds, toasted	flaked almonds, toasted

Divide ratafias between 4 sundae glasses and sprinkle each with one tablespoon of whiskey. Drain apricots, reserve 4 for decoration, roughly chop the remainder and use to cover ratafias. In the top of a double boiler beat the eggs with the sugar, then stir in the hot but not boiling milk. Cook over boiling water, stirring frequently, until the custard thickens sufficiently to coat the spoon. Remove from heat and cool a little before spooning over apricots. Leave until cold. To serve, cover each trifle with lightly whipped cream and decorate with reserved apricots and flaked almonds.

Italian cream cheese cups

Serves: 4

IMPERIAL	METRIC	AMERICAN
8 oz. cream cheese	225 g. cream cheese	1 cup cream cheese
2 oz. castor sugar	50 g. castor sugar	¼ cup granulated sugar
2 eggs, separated	2 eggs, separated	2 eggs, separated
1–2 tablespoons brandy, Kirsch *or* orange liqueur	1–2 tablespoons brandy, Kirsch *or* orange liqueur	1–3 tablespoons brandy, Kirsch *or* orange liqueur
8 oz. raspberries *or* small strawberries*	225 g. raspberries *or* small strawberries*	1½ cups raspberries *or* small strawberries*
savoy biscuits	savoy biscuits	ladyfingers

Press the cream cheese through a strainer into a basin. Add the sugar and egg yolks and beat until light and fluffy. Flavour to taste with liqueur. Whisk the egg whites until stiff then fold lightly but thoroughly into the cream. Pile into individual glasses and stud the surface with raspberries or strawberries. Serve with savoy biscuits.
*Ideally, fresh or dry frozen raspberries, or wild strawberries.

Tipsy hedgehog

Cooking time: 25–30 minutes
Temperature: 350°F., 180°C.,
   Gas Mark 4
Serves: 6–8

IMPERIAL	METRIC	AMERICAN
sponge cake base	*sponge cake base*	*sponge cake base*
2 large eggs	2 large eggs	2 eggs
4 oz. castor sugar	110 g. castor sugar	½ cup granulated sugar
3 oz. plain flour, sifted	85 g. plain flour, sifted	¾ cup all-purpose flour, sifted
to assemble	*to assemble*	*to assemble*
½ pint orange wine	3 dl. orange wine	1¼ cups orange wine
2 tablespoons sieved apricot jam	2 tablespoons sieved apricot jam	3 tablespoons sieved apricot jam
powdered drinking chocolate	powdered drinking chocolate	sweetened cocoa powder
3 oz. blanched almonds	85 g. blanched almonds	¾ cup blanched almonds
1 glacé cherry	1 glacé cherry	1 candied cherry
½ pint whipping cream	3 dl. whipping cream	1¼ cups whipping cream
1 tablespoon castor sugar	1 tablespoon castor sugar	1 tablespoon granulated sugar

A charming eighteenth century frivolity for special occasions. Make the sponge several days in advance so that it stales a little. Have the ingredients for the cake at room temperature. Line a 2-lb. loaf tin with greaseproof paper and brush with oil. Preheat the oven. Break the eggs into a mixing bowl, add the sugar and whisk together steadily until the mixture is *very* thick and mousse-like. Fold in the sifted flour and when evenly mixed turn into the prepared tin. Bake in centre of oven until well risen and springy to the touch. Cool on a wire rack. To assemble the hedgehog, cut off corners of sponge, round the top and taper towards one end representing the shape of a hedgehog. Place on an oval serving dish. Cut a wedge from top of sponge and fill with the wine, repeating as absorbed until all the wine is used and the sponge and wedge soaked through and through. Replace wedge. With a pastry brush dab the sponge all over with warmed apricot jam and then sprinkle *thickly* with drinking chocolate powder. Split the almonds lengthways into thin strips and spike the sponge closely all over, sloping the almond slivers backwards to resemble the prickles of a hedgehog. Cut the cherry in half and arrange as two beady eyes. Whip the cream, sweeten with the sugar, and arrange in swirls, piped or spooned, all around the base of the hedgehog.

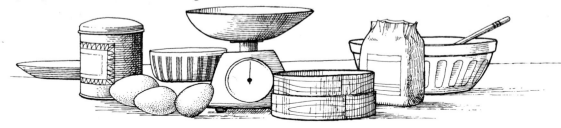

Old fashioned orange creams

Serves: 4

IMPERIAL	METRIC	AMERICAN
1 large orange	1 large orange	1 large orange
½ small lemon	½ small lemon	½ small lemon
2 oz. castor sugar	50 g. castor sugar	¼ cup granulated sugar
1 tablespoon brandy *or* orange liqueur	1 tablespoon brandy *or* orange liqueur	1 tablespoon brandy *or* orange liqueur
2 egg yolks	2 egg yolks	2 egg yolks
¼ pint double cream	1½ dl. double cream	⅔ cup whipping cream

A delicate and delicious eighteenth century recipe which must then have taken hours to make but now requires 10 minutes in an electric blender. First pare the orange and lemon rind with a potato peeler, cover with water and boil for 10 minutes. Drain.

Put into an electric blender with strained orange and lemon juice, and the sugar. Blend at high speed until rinds are pulverised. Add the brandy or liqueur and egg yolks and blend thoroughly. Heat the cream to boiling point and add gradually to the orange mixture, blending at low speed until a smooth thick cream is formed. When cool pour into custard glasses and serve with boudoir biscuits.

Pineapple fritters (see recipe on page 67)

Savarin chantilly

Cooking time: about 20 minutes
Temperature: 400°F., 200°C., Gas Mark 6
Serves: 4–5

IMPERIAL	METRIC	AMERICAN
4½ oz. plain flour	125 g. plain flour	1 cup plus 2 tablespoons all-purpose flour
¼ oz. fresh yeast	10 g. fresh yeast	½ tablespoon active dry yeast
4 tablespoons milk	4 tablespoons milk	⅓ cup milk
2 eggs	2 eggs	2 eggs
1½ oz. softened butter	40 g. softened butter	3 tablespoons softened butter
1 teaspoon sugar	1 teaspoon sugar	1 teaspoon sugar
pinch salt	pinch salt	pinch salt
syrup	*syrup*	*syrup*
4 oz. sugar	100 g. sugar	½ cup sugar
¼ pint water	1½ dl. water	⅔ cup water
2–3 tablespoons rum or Kirsch	2–3 tablespoons rum or Kirsch	3–4 tablespoons rum or Kirsch
glaze (optional)	*glaze (optional)*	*glaze (optional)*
3 tablespoons sieved apricot jam	3 tablespoons sieved apricot jam	¼ cup sieved apricot jam
1 tablespoon water	1 tablespoon water	1 tablespoon water
to decorate	*to decorate*	*to decorate*
¼ pint double cream	1½ dl. double cream	⅔ cup whipping cream
candied *or* canned fruit	candied *or* canned fruit	candied *or* canned fruit

Sift flour into a warm bowl and make a 'well' in the centre. Dissolve yeast in warm milk, add lightly beaten eggs, and pour into flour. With one hand mix until smooth (the mixture is a soft and sticky one) then beat thoroughly for 4 to 5 minutes. Cover basin and set to rise in warm place about 40 minutes or until doubled in bulk. When dough is risen add the butter, sugar and salt and beat by hand for 4 to 5 minutes. Turn into a greased 7-inch (18-cm.) ring mould, cover, and leave to prove for 15 minutes or until mixture rises to top of tin. Bake towards top of preheated oven for about 20 minutes until firm and brown.

To make syrup, dissolve sugar in water then simmer for 3 minutes; add the rum or Kirsch. Turn savarin upside down on a cooling rack; after 5 minutes loosen with a knife and turn into a shallow serving dish. Immediately spoon the warm syrup over, little by little, until sponge is moist throughout and the syrup absorbed. To glaze, heat apricot purée and water together, then brush liberally over the sponge. When cold, and shortly before serving, whip and sweeten cream to taste and pile in the centre of savarin and decorate with candied or drained canned fruits.

Dean's cream

Serves: 6–8

IMPERIAL	METRIC	AMERICAN
1 packet trifle sponge cakes (8 sponges)	1 packet trifle sponge cakes (8 sponges)	16 ladyfingers
little raspberry jam	little raspberry jam	little raspberry jam
little orange marmalade	little orange marmalade	little orange marmalade
some ratafia biscuits	some ratafia biscuits	some ratafias *or* small macaroons
¼ pint sweet sherry	1½ dl. sweet sherry	⅔ cup sweet sherry
¼ pint fruit juice	1½ dl. fruit juice	⅔ cup fruit juice
2 tablespoons icing sugar or to taste	2 tablespoons icing sugar or to taste	3 tablespoons confectioners' sugar or to taste
4 tablespoons brandy	4 tablespoons brandy	⅓ cup brandy
¾ pint double cream	4½ dl. double cream	scant 2 cups heavy cream
glacé fruits and ratafias	glacé fruits and ratafias	candied fruits and ratafias

A gloriously rich trifle of the eighteenth century, when it was a favourite pudding at Cambridge University. Split the sponge cakes, spread half with raspberry jam and half with orange marmalade. Arrange alternately in a glass trifle dish. Add some ratafias. Pour over the mixed sherry and fruit juice to soak the sponge evenly.

Add the icing sugar and brandy to the cream and whip steadily until very thick. Pour over the soaked sponge and allow to stand for an hour or two. Decorate with pieces of colourful glacé fruit and ratafias. This trifle has quite a kick!

Chocolate bombe

Cooking time: 35–40 minutes
Temperature: 325°F., 170°C.,
    Gas Mark 3
Serves: 4–5

IMPERIAL	METRIC	AMERICAN
sponge	*sponge*	*sponge*
2 oz. castor sugar	50 g. castor sugar	$\frac{1}{4}$ cup granulated sugar
2 large eggs	2 large eggs	2 eggs
2 oz. self-raising flour	50 g. self-raising flour	$\frac{1}{2}$ cup all-purpose flour sifted with $\frac{1}{2}$ teaspoon baking powder
1 tablespoon cocoa	1 tablespoon cocoa	1 tablespoon cocoa
sauce	*sauce*	*sauce*
1 tablespoon cocoa	1 tablespoon cocoa	1 tablespoon cocoa
1 tablespoon sugar	1 tablespoon sugar	1 tablespoon sugar
$\frac{1}{4}$ pint boiling water	$1\frac{1}{2}$ dl. boiling water	$\frac{2}{3}$ cup boiling water
2 tablespoons rum	2 tablespoons rum	3 tablespoons rum
2 tablespoons orange squash	2 tablespoons orange squash	3 tablespoons orange drink
to decorate	*to decorate*	*to decorate*
$\frac{1}{4}$ pint double cream	$1\frac{1}{2}$ dl. double cream	$\frac{3}{4}$ cup heavy cream
2 tablespoons milk	2 tablespoons milk	3 tablespoons milk
2 teaspoons icing sugar	2 teaspoons icing sugar	2 teaspoons confectioners' sugar
coarsely grated chocolate	coarsely grated chocolate	coarsely grated chocolate

Preheat oven and warm the sugar. Butter an oven-proof glass pudding basin. Put the warmed sugar and eggs into a mixing bowl and whisk until *very* thick and mousse-like. Lightly but thoroughly fold in the sifted flour and cocoa. Turn into the prepared basin and bake in centre of oven until well risen and firm to the touch. Turn out on to a plate.

For the sauce put the cocoa and sugar into a small pan, stir in the boiling water and cook, stirring, for 1 to 2 minutes, then add the rum and orange squash. Immediately start pouring, a spoonful at a time, over the hot sponge, until all the sauce is absorbed. Leave until cold. Shortly before serving whisk the cream and milk together until thick then stir in the sugar. Carefully spread the whipped cream all over the sponge, and sprinkle lightly with grated chocolate.

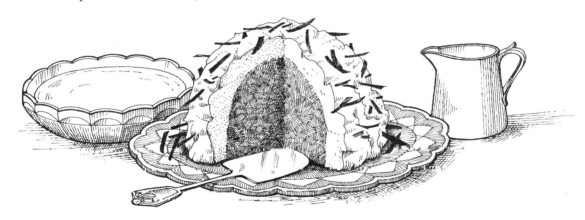

Scotch mist

Serves: 4–5

IMPERIAL	METRIC	AMERICAN
1 large egg white	1 large egg white	1 egg white
$\frac{1}{2}$ pint double cream	3 dl. double cream	$1\frac{1}{4}$ cups heavy cream
4 tablespoons Drambuie	4 tablespoons Drambuie	$\frac{1}{3}$ cup Drambuie
2 tablespoons clear heather honey	2 tablespoons clear heather honey	3 tablespoons clear heather honey

Whisk the egg white until stiff. In another basin whisk the cream, Drambuie and honey together until thick. Fold egg white lightly but thoroughly into the cream mixture. Transfer to small individual glasses, and if possible leave to stand for several hours for the flavours to blend. Serve with thin shortbread or petticoat-tail biscuits.

Strawberry flan chantilly

Cooking time: 20–25 minutes
Temperature: 400°F., 200°C.,
 Gas Mark 6
Serves: 4–6

IMPERIAL	METRIC	AMERICAN
rich shortcrust	*rich shortcrust*	*rich pie crust*
6 oz. plain flour	175 g. plain flour	1½ cups all-purpose flour
¼ teaspoon salt	¼ teaspoon salt	¼ teaspoon salt
1 tablespoon castor sugar	1 tablespoon castor sugar	1 tablespoon granulated sugar
3 oz. lard	85 g. lard	6 tablespoons lard
1 egg yolk	1 egg yolk	1 egg yolk
filling	*filling*	*filling*
1 lb. firm strawberries	450 g. firm strawberries	1 lb. firm strawberries
castor sugar	castor sugar	granulated sugar
4 tablespoons Grand Marnier	4 tablespoons Grand Marnier	⅓ cup Grand Marnier
1 large egg white	1 large egg white	1 egg white
½ pint double cream	3 dl. double cream	1¼ cups heavy cream

For the shortcrust, sieve flour, salt and sugar into a bowl and rub in lard until the mixture resembles fine breadcrumbs. Mix to a stiffish dough with the egg yolk and if necessary a few drops of cold water. Roll out thinly and line an 8-inch (20-cm.) flan ring. Prick base well and line closely with foil. Bake in preheated oven for 15 minutes; then remove foil and continue cooking until flan is baked. Leave until cold.

For the filling, reserve a dozen good berries for decorating. Slice remainder, dust liberally with sugar and add the liqueur. Stir, and leave in a cold place for 30 minutes or so. When ready to fill the flan, whisk egg white until stiff. Whisk cream until stiff and put one-third aside for decorating. Fold sliced strawberries and their liquid into remaining cream followed by the beaten egg white. Pile into the flan case. Decorate with reserved strawberries, and the cream.

Cold orange soufflé

Serves: 4–5

IMPERIAL	METRIC	AMERICAN
3 large eggs, separated	3 large eggs, separated	3 eggs, separated
2 oz. castor sugar	50 g. castor sugar	¼ cup granulated sugar
5 tablespoons concentrated frozen orange juice	5 tablespoons concentrated frozen orange juice	6 tablespoons concentrated frozen orange juice
2 tablespoons Cointreau	2 tablespoons Cointreau	2–3 tablespoons Cointreau
1 teaspoon lemon juice	1 teaspoon lemon juice	1 teaspoon lemon juice
2 tablespoons water	2 tablespoons water	3 tablespoons water
½ oz. gelatine	15 g. gelatine	2 envelopes gelatin
¼ pint double cream	1½ dl. double cream	⅔ cup heavy cream
to decorate	*to decorate*	*to decorate*
chocolate vermicelli	chocolate vermicelli	chocolate vermicelli *or* grated chocolate
whipped cream	whipped cream	whipped cream
1 orange slice	1 orange slice	1 candied orange slice

Prepare a 5-inch (13-cm.) soufflé dish with a collar of greaseproof paper tied around the outside to reach 3 inches (7½ cm.) above the rim. Put the egg yolks and sugar into a large bowl and rest the bowl over a pan of gently boiling water. Whisk the mixture until thick and creamy. Remove from heat and whisk in orange juice, Cointreau and lemon juice. Put the 2 tablespoons water in a small cup, sprinkle in the gelatine and dissolve by standing the cup in a pan of hot water. When clear, stir in orange mixture. Cool until just beginning to set.

Whisk the cream until thick and fold gently into the mixture, followed by the stiffly beaten egg whites. Pour immediately into the prepared soufflé case, and leave to set in a cool place. To serve, remove paper collar and coat sides with chocolate vermicelli. Pipe a little cream around edge and arrange small pieces of orange slice in the centre.

Apples flamed with rum (see recipe on page 10)

Hot puddings

In spite of the present vogue for fruit and cheese to end a meal, many people have a sneaking affection for a good hot pudding, especially in cold weather.

This chapter includes a wide variety of puddings in which a spoonful or so of wine, spirit or liqueur gives a noticeable lift to the flavour. Ideas range from quickly prepared yet slightly exotic fruit dishes such as Calypso caramel oranges or Barbados baked bananas to the Omelette soufflé au liqueur of restaurant fame but which is by no means beyond the scope of a good home cook. For dining à deux, this soufflé omelette will make your guest feel very pampered especially if you flame it. Then for the really hungry there are more substantial favourites such as Pudding Celestine and Raisin and rum flan.

Barbados baked bananas

Cooking time: about 20 minutes
Temperature: 375°F., 190°C., Gas Mark 5
Serves: 4

IMPERIAL	METRIC	AMERICAN
8 small *or* 4 large firm bananas	8 small *or* 4 large firm bananas	8 small *or* 4 large firm bananas
1½ oz. butter	40 g. butter	3 tablespoons butter
juice of 1 lemon	juice of 1 lemon	juice of 1 lemon
3 tablespoons shredded coconut	3 tablespoons shredded coconut	¼ cup shredded coconut
3 tablespoons soft brown sugar	3 tablespoons soft brown sugar	¼ cup soft brown sugar
3 tablespoons rum	3 tablespoons rum	¼ cup rum

Peel bananas and if large ones cut in half across. Lay side by side in a buttered ovenproof dish so that they fit fairly closely. Sprinkle them evenly with the lemon juice, then with coconut, then with sugar and finally with the rum. Dot remaining butter over the surface and bake in the centre of preheated oven.

The dish is ready when the bananas are soft and the surface deep golden. Serve with thin cream. If you are feeling extravagant pour an extra tablespoon of rum into a warmed spoon, ignite, and serve the bananas aflame.

Raisin and rum flan

Cooking time: 30–35 minutes
Temperature: 350°F., 180°C., Gas Mark 4
Serves: 4–5

IMPERIAL	METRIC	AMERICAN
1 baked 8-inch flan case	1 baked 20-cm. flan case	1 baked 8-inch pie shell
3 oz. raisins*	75 g. raisins*	⅔ cup raisins*
2 tablespoons rum	2 tablespoons rum	3 tablespoons rum
little milk	little milk	little milk
1 tablespoon cornflour	1 tablespoon cornflour	1 tablespoon cornstarch
2 oz. sugar	50 g. sugar	¼ cup sugar
1 egg, separated	1 egg, separated	1 egg, separated
¼ pint single cream	1½ dl. single cream	⅔ cup coffee cream

Soak the raisins in the rum for at least 2 hours. Preheat the oven. Strain liquor from raisins and make up a scant ¼ pint with milk. Mix together the cornflour, sugar and egg yolk and stir in the milk and cream, mixing thoroughly. Fold in the stiffly whisked egg white. Pour gently into the flan case and sprinkle in two-thirds of raisins.

Bake in centre of oven for 15 minutes, then press remaining raisins into slightly set surface. Continue cooking another 15 to 20 minutes, until set. Serve hot or cold.

*Use seeded raisins if available, otherwise seedless.

Austrian wine pudding

Cooking time: 20–25 minutes
Temperature: 375°F., 190°C.,
   Gas Mark 5
Serves: 4

IMPERIAL	METRIC	AMERICAN
pudding	*pudding*	*pudding*
1½ oz. ground nuts, preferably unblanched*	40 g. ground nuts, preferably unblanched*	⅓ cup ground nuts, preferably unblanched*
¾ oz. biscuit crumbs	20 g. biscuit crumbs	3 tablespoons cookie crumbs
3 eggs, separated	3 eggs, separated	3 eggs, separated
1½ oz. castor sugar	40 g. castor sugar	3 tablespoons sugar
1 teaspoon grated lemon rind	1 teaspoon grated lemon rind	1 teaspoon grated lemon rind
syrup	*syrup*	*syrup*
2½ oz. castor sugar	65 g. castor sugar	⅓ cup granulated sugar
4 tablespoons water	4 tablespoons water	⅓ cup water
¼ pint medium or sweet white wine	1½ dl. medium or sweet white wine	⅔ cup medium or sweet white wine
1 clove	1 clove	1 clove
rind and juice of ½ lemon	rind and juice of ½ lemon	rind and juice of ½ lemon

Grind the nuts and biscuits in a coffee mill or electric blender. Butter a deep pie or soufflé dish. Put the egg yolks and half the sugar into a mixing bowl. In another basin whisk the egg whites until stiff, add the remaining sugar and whisk until again stiff. Beat the egg yolks and sugar until pale and creamy, then lightly fold in the egg whites, nuts, crumbs and lemon rind. Turn into the dish and bake in centre of preheated oven until risen, firm and golden brown.

Meanwhile prepare the syrup. Melt the sugar in a small saucepan with 2 tablespoons of the water and when quite dissolved boil briskly until beginning to caramelise. Off the heat add the remaining water, the wine, clove and pared lemon rind. Simmer for 2 minutes. When ready to serve add lemon juice and strain the syrup over the pudding, which will promptly absorb it. Serve at once.

*Any nuts will do; hazelnuts are especially good.

Calypso caramel oranges

Cooking time: 20–25 minutes
Temperature: 325°F., 170°C.,
   Gas Mark 3
Serves: 3

IMPERIAL	METRIC	AMERICAN
4 large oranges	4 large oranges	4 large oranges
8 teaspoons orange liqueur *or* rum	8 teaspoons orange liqueur *or* rum	8 teaspoons orange liqueur *or* rum
little castor sugar	little castor sugar	little granulated sugar
to decorate	*to decorate*	*to decorate*
glacé cherries	glacé cherries	candied cherries

Use thin-skinned oranges, preferably seedless. Cut the oranges in half horizontally. Use a grapefruit knife to remove central core and loosen the segments. Arrange oranges cut side up on a shallow flameproof serving dish and carefully pour a teaspoon of liqueur or rum over each. Cook in the centre of a preheated oven for 15 minutes.

Sprinkle the surface of each orange thickly with sugar, and put under a low grill to first melt and then caramelise the sugar to a deep golden brown. Allow to cool a little before serving with a glacé cherry in the centre of each. If you have some handy, decorate the serving dish with glossy green leaves.

Omelette soufflé au liqueur

Cooking time: 2–3 minutes
Serves: 2

IMPERIAL	METRIC	AMERICAN
2 large eggs, separated	2 large eggs, separated	2 eggs, separated
1 oz. castor sugar	25 g. castor sugar	2 tablespoons granulated sugar
finely grated rind of ½ orange	finely grated rind of ½ orange	finely grated rind of ½ orange
2 tablespoons liqueur (see method)	2 tablespoons liqueur (see method)	3 tablespoons liqueur (see method)
½ oz. butter	15 g. butter	1 tablespoon butter
castor sugar for dusting	castor sugar for dusting	granulated sugar for dusting

You can either make one large omelette in a heavy 10-inch (25-cm.) pan or two individual ones in a 7-inch (17½-cm.) pan. Beat together egg yolks, sugar, rind and liqueur (Grand Marnier, Cointreau, apricot brandy, etc.) until pale and creamy. Start heating the omelette pan gently. Whisk egg whites until very stiff, then fold lightly into the yolks.

Variations

Omelette soufflé au rhum
Omit liqueur, instead add 1 tablespoon creamy milk to yolk mixture. As soon as the omelette is cooked spread with hot rather runny apricot jam, fold, and dish on a heatproof plate. Heat 2 to 3 tablespoons rum, ignite and pour flaming around omelette.

Heat butter in pan and when foaming pour in the mixture and spread evenly. Cook over *moderate* heat for 1 to 1½ minutes to set the underside, then slip under a preheated *moderate* grill and cook another 1 to 1½ minutes until lightly set. Slide on to a hot dish, folding the omelette in half as you do so. Sprinkle with sugar and serve immediately.

Omelette soufflé Martinique
Substitute banana slices fried in butter for the jam, and finish with rum as opposite.

Pudding Celestine

Cooking time: 1½–2 hours
Serves: 4

IMPERIAL	METRIC	AMERICAN
4 oz. butter	110 g. butter	½ cup butter
4 oz. castor sugar	110 g. castor sugar	½ cup granulated sugar
finely grated rind of 1 orange and ½ lemon	finely grated rind of 1 orange and ½ lemon	finely grated rind of 1 orange and ½ lemon
2 eggs	2 eggs	2 eggs
4 oz. plain flour	110 g. plain flour	1 cup all-purpose flour
1 teaspoon baking powder	1 teaspoon baking powder	1 teaspoon baking powder
1 oz. fine breadcrumbs	25 g. fine breadcrumbs	¼ cup fine bread crumbs
3 oz. chopped glacé cherries	85 g. chopped glacé cherries	½ cup chopped candied cherries
3–4 tablespoons milk	3–4 tablespoons milk	¼–⅓ cup milk
to serve	*to serve*	*to serve*
Madeira foam sauce (see page 25) *or* Curaçao	Madeira foam sauce (see page 25) *or* Curaçao	Madeira foam sauce (see page 25) *or* Curaçao

Prepare a steamer. Butter a heatproof basin and a square of greaseproof or foil to cover it. Cream the butter at room temperature with the sugar, grated orange and lemon rind until light and fluffy. Beat in the eggs. Gently stir in the flour sifted with the baking powder, the breadcrumbs and glacé cherries. Mix to a soft dropping consistency with milk. Turn into the prepared basin, cover closely and steam for 1½ to 2 hours.

Turn out and serve with Madeira foam sauce poured over it. Or in the words of the original nineteenth century cook '. . . pour a wineglass of Curaçao under it and serve'.

Brandy snaps (see recipe on page 72)

Fruit desserts

Fresh fruit is such a welcome ending to a meal that one wonders whether the addition of wine is merely gilding the lily. But for occasions when plain fruit seems a shade pedestrian, or a glut has led to monotony, a little wine can be the answer. When, for instance, the first flush of strawberries or peaches is over, try macerating them in wine (see below).

Fruit liqueurs are especially successful in adding an extra flavour dimension, but proceed with caution as too generous a dose can overwhelm the natural flavour. Golden rum is a wonderful flavour with apples, bananas, oranges and pineapple and can transform a quite ordinary dish – apple fritters for instance – into something special.

Peaches in red or white wine

Serves: 4

IMPERIAL	METRIC	AMERICAN
4–8 ripe peaches	4–8 ripe peaches	4–8 ripe peaches
sifted icing sugar	sifted icing sugar	sifted confectioners' sugar
½ bottle red or white wine	½ bottle red or white wine	½ bottle red or white wine

Pour boiling water over the peaches, leave for a minute, then skin them. Slice, and divide them evenly between 4 large wine glasses. Depending on the dryness or sweetness of the wine used, add sugar to taste and cover the peaches with the wine. Leave to stand for at least half an hour before serving, preferably slightly chilled.

Variation
Strawberries in wine
Replace the sliced peaches with 1½ lb. whole ripe hulled strawberries. Leave to stand for 1 to 2 hours before serving.

Summer fruit salad

Serves: 4

IMPERIAL	METRIC	AMERICAN
2 ripe peaches	2 ripe peaches	2 ripe peaches
2 ripe pears	2 ripe pears	2 ripe pears
2 tablespoons lemon juice	2 tablespoons lemon juice	3 tablespoons lemon juice
3 ripe apricots	3 ripe apricots	3 ripe apricots
3 ripe plums	3 ripe plums	3 ripe plums
1–2 tablespoons Maraschino, Kirsch or Strega	1–2 tablespoons Maraschino, Kirsch or Strega	2–3 tablespoons Maraschino, Kirsch or Strega
3–4 tablespoons castor sugar	3–4 tablespoons castor sugar	¼–⅓ cup granulated sugar
few raspberries or strawberries	few raspberries or strawberries	few raspberries or strawberries

Skin the peaches and pears and cut into small slices. Put into a bowl with the lemon juice and turn over and over to prevent browning. Slice the apricots and plums and add with the liqueur and sugar. Mix thoroughly, cover and leave in a cool place for several hours, during which time the sugar will dissolve and form a syrup with the fruit juices.

Just before serving add the raspberries or strawberries. Serve in shallow glass dishes, and preferably without cream so that the lovely fresh fruit flavours can be appreciated.

Winter fruit salad

Cooking time: 5 minutes
Serves: 4

IMPERIAL	METRIC	AMERICAN
2 crisp dessert apples	2 crisp dessert apples	2 crisp dessert apples
2 dessert pears	2 dessert pears	2 dessert pears
2 bananas	2 bananas	2 bananas
4–6 oz. grapes, black *or* green	100–175 g. grapes, black *or* green	1–1½ cups grapes, purple *or* green
2 large oranges	2 large oranges	2 large oranges
syrup	*syrup*	*syrup*
¼ pint water	1½ dl. water	⅔ cup water
4 oz. castor sugar	100 g. castor sugar	½ cup granulated sugar
thinly pared rind of ½ orange	thinly pared rind of ½ orange	thinly pared rind of ½ orange
juice of 1 lemon	juice of 1 lemon	juice of 1 lemon
1 tablespoon orange liqueur	1 tablespoon orange liqueur	1 tablespoon orange liqueur

Make the syrup and allow to cool before adding the fruit. Heat the water, sugar and orange rind together gently until sugar dissolves, then boil steadily for 3 minutes. When cold add the lemon juice and liqueur and strain into a glass bowl.

Prepare the apples, pears and bananas and slice into the syrup, turning over and over so that each slice is coated with syrup to prevent discolouration. Halve and de-seed the grapes. With a sharp knife cut the peel off the oranges, removing the white skin at the same time, then cut segments free of skin and add to the salad. Chill for an hour or so before serving, preferably *without* cream.

Strawberries Romanoff

Serves: 4

IMPERIAL	METRIC	AMERICAN
1½ lb. strawberries	700 g. strawberries	1½ lb. strawberries
1 large *or* 2 small oranges	1 large *or* 2 small oranges	1 large *or* 2 small oranges
1½ oz. lump sugar	40 g. lump sugar	¼ cup lump sugar
3 tablespoons Curaçao *or* Grand Marnier	3 tablespoons Curaçao *or* Grand Marnier	¼ cup Curaçao *or* Grand Marnier
whipped fresh cream	whipped fresh cream	whipped fresh cream

Hull the strawberries and put into a deep bowl. Wash the oranges and rub some of the sugar lumps over the skin to extract the yellow zest. Place all the sugar lumps in a small bowl, add the squeezed orange juice and hasten the dissolving process by crushing the sugar with a wooden spoon. Add the liqueur. Pour this syrup over the strawberries, cover and leave in a cool place for at least an hour. Serve in coupe glasses with a swirl of whipped cream on top.

Cherries in red wine

Cooking time: about 15 minutes
Serves: 4

IMPERIAL	METRIC	AMERICAN
4 oz. sugar	100 g. sugar	½ cup sugar
pinch powdered cinnamon	pinch powdered cinnamon	pinch powdered cinnamon
thin strip orange peel	thin strip orange peel	thin strip orange peel
1 tablespoon redcurrant jelly	1 tablespoon redcurrant jelly	1 tablespoon red currant jelly
¼ pint robust red wine	1½ dl. robust red wine	⅔ cup robust red wine
1 lb. large ripe cherries, preferably Morello	450 g. large ripe cherries, preferably Morello	1 lb. large ripe cherries, preferably Bing

In Italy the wine traditionally used for this recipe is Barolo, a wine as big and full bodied as its name. A robust Burgundy could be used instead. Put the sugar, cinnamon, orange peel, jelly and wine in a saucepan and heat gently until sugar has dissolved, then boil for 1 minute. Add the cherries (stoned if you have time), and simmer for 10 minutes or until cooked.

Transfer cherries to a serving dish, reduce the syrup by rapid boiling for several minutes, then strain over the cherries. Served chilled.

Orange délice

Serves: 3

IMPERIAL	METRIC	AMERICAN
3 tablespoons orange juice	3 tablespoons orange juice	¼ cup orange juice
2 oz. icing sugar	50 g. icing sugar	¼ cup confectioners' sugar
1 tablespoon orange liqueur (Grand Marnier, Curaçao)	1 tablespoon orange liqueur (Grand Marnier, Curaçao)	1 tablespoon orange liqueur (Grand Marnier, Curaçao)
¼ pint double cream	1½ dl. double cream	⅔ cup heavy cream
1 large egg white	1 large egg white	1 egg white

Put the first four ingredients into a basin and whisk together until thick enough to stand in soft peaks. Whisk the egg white until stiff and fold lightly but evenly into the orange cream. Pile into glasses and serve with boudoir biscuits.

Pears Marsala

Cooking time: about 30 minutes
Serves: 4

IMPERIAL	METRIC	AMERICAN
6 oz. sugar	175 g. sugar	¾ cup sugar
1 pint water	generous ½ litre water	2½ cups water
4 large pears	4 large pears	4 large pears
apricot glaze	*apricot glaze*	*apricot glaze*
6 tablespoons apricot jam	6 tablespoons apricot jam	½ cup apricot jam
2 tablespoons Marsala *or* Madeira	2 tablespoons Marsala *or* Madeira	3 tablespoons Marsala *or* Madeira
little lemon juice	little lemon juice	little lemon juice
to decorate	*to decorate*	*to decorate*
toasted flaked almonds	toasted flaked almonds	toasted flaked almonds

Make a syrup by dissolving the sugar in the water and boiling for several minutes. Peel, halve and core the pears and poach very gently in the syrup for 20 to 30 minutes, until tender. Meanwhile heat the apricot jam with the wine, then press through a strainer. Add a little lemon juice to sharpen the flavour and if necessary a little of the poaching syrup to thin the sauce to a coating consistency. Drain the pears, arrange in a serving dish, coat with the glaze and sprinkle with the almonds.

Barnstaple fair pears

Cooking time: 4–6 hours
Temperature: 275°F., 140°C., Gas Mark 1
Serves: 6

IMPERIAL	METRIC	AMERICAN
½ pint water	3 dl. water	1¼ cups water
¼ pint port	1½ dl. port	⅔ cup port
12 oz. granulated sugar	350 g. granulated sugar	1½ cups granulated sugar
1 small lemon	1 small lemon	1 small lemon
2 cloves	2 cloves	2 cloves
1-inch piece stick cinnamon	2·5-cm. piece stick cinnamon	1-inch piece stick cinnamon
2 lb. hard cooking pears	1 kg. hard cooking pears	2 lb. hard cooking pears

If you are fortunate enough to come by some really hard cooking pears, do as our grandmothers did and bake them long and very slowly in port-flavoured syrup. The resulting mahogany coloured pears were a speciality of Barnstaple fair.

Put water, port, sugar, *thinly* pared lemon rind, lemon juice and spices into a pan and heat gently until dissolved. Meanwhile peel, halve and core pears and drop them into the hot syrup. Bring to the boil, transfer to a deep casserole, cover tightly and cook in a slow oven until tender. The time will vary from 4 to 6 hours, depending on the pears, but cooking can be spread over several days if more convenient. Serve cold, with clotted cream.

Elysian apple fritters

Cooking time: 3–4 minutes
Serves: 3–4

IMPERIAL	METRIC	AMERICAN
3 large dessert apples	3 large dessert apples	3 large dessert apples
2 oz. castor sugar	50 g. castor sugar	¼ cup granulated sugar
4 tablespoons apple wine, Calvados, rum or brandy	4 tablespoons apple wine, Calvados, rum or brandy	⅓ cup apple wine, Calvados, rum or brandy
oil for frying	oil for frying	oil for frying
batter	*batter*	*batter*
2 oz. plain flour, sifted	50 g. plain flour, sifted	½ cup all-purpose flour, sifted
large pinch salt	large pinch salt	large pinch salt
2 teaspoons vegetable oil	2 teaspoons vegetable oil	2 teaspoons vegetable oil
3–4 tablespoons tepid water	3–4 tablespoons tepid water	¼–⅓ cup tepid water
1 egg white	1 egg white	1 egg white

Peel and core the apples. Cut into ¼-inch (½-cm.) rings and put into a shallow dish sprinkling each layer with sugar. Pour over the wine or spirit and leave to steep for at least 30 minutes, turning now and then.

In a basin mix the flour, salt, oil and water to a smooth batter of coating consistency. Leave until ready to fry the fritters, then fold in the stiffly whisked egg white. Heat a pan of oil until hot enough to brown a piece of bread in 40 seconds (about 340°F., 172°C.). Dip the apple slices one at a time into the batter and immediately lower into the hot oil. Cook until golden and crisp, turning once. Drain on absorbent paper. Serve sprinkled with remaining 'soaking' juices, and dredge with castor sugar.

Variation
Pineapple fritters (illustrated on page 55)
Steep fresh pineapple slices or rings in sugar and Kirsch; for canned slices omit the sugar. If liked, serve with jam.

Melon and ginger coupes

Serves: 4

IMPERIAL	METRIC	AMERICAN
1 small ripe honeydew melon	1 small ripe honeydew melon	1 small ripe honeydew melon
about ¼ pint ginger wine	about 1½ dl. ginger wine	about ⅔ cup ginger wine
2 tablespoons castor sugar	2 tablespoons castor sugar	3 tablespoons granulated sugar
about 1 tablespoon lemon juice	about 1 tablespoon lemon juice	about 1 tablespoon lemon juice
to decorate	*to decorate*	*to decorate*
whipped fresh cream	whipped fresh cream	whipped fresh cream
slices preserved ginger	slices preserved ginger	slices preserved ginger

Slice the top off the melon about one-quarter of the way down from the top. With a spoon scoop out and discard the seeds. Fill the cavity with ginger wine and add the sugar. Cover with the 'lid' and leave in a refrigerator or cold larder overnight.

Shortly before serving drain the wine into a bowl. Quarter the melon, cut the flesh into dice and add to the ginger wine with lemon juice and sugar to taste. Serve in coupe glasses topped with whipped cream and decorated with a slice of preserved ginger.
Note. If ginger wine is not available, it may be replaced by sweet sherry and 3–4 tablespoons chopped preserved ginger.

Ice creams and sorbets

Ambrosia is the only word to describe these home-made liqueur-flavoured ices. And far from being troublesome to make, most of the recipes in this chapter could not be simpler. Many manage to avoid completely that tiresome business of being turned out of the tray for whisking when half frozen. Only with sorbets does this process seem unavoidable.

For freezing ices, follow any directions given by the manufacturer of your refrigerator. If the frozen food compartment in your refrigerator is marked with *one* star, indicating a temperature of around 21°F., —6°C., several of the ices will not freeze firmly. But try them because they are still delicious.

The lower the freezing temperature the harder your ice will freeze. So with two or three star refrigerators or home freezers, remember to remove the ice to the main part of the refrigerator about 30 minutes before serving so that it can soften gradually to a pleasant temperature and texture for eating.

Of course, you do not *have* to make an ice. Almost any liqueur is delicious just poured over bought ice cream or sorbet, about a tablespoon per portion. This offers an opportunity to try some of the more unusual liqueur flavours such as Anisette (aniseed), Kummel (caraway), Crème de menthe (peppermint), Advocaat (egg and brandy), or Strega (herbs).

Orange liqueur sorbet

Serves: 4

IMPERIAL	METRIC	AMERICAN
2 oz. sugar	50 g. sugar	$\frac{1}{4}$ cup sugar
$\frac{1}{2}$ pint water	3 dl. water	$1\frac{1}{4}$ cups water
$\frac{1}{4}$ oz. powdered gelatine	10 g. powdered gelatine	1 envelope gelatin
$6\frac{1}{4}$-fl. oz. can frozen orange juice	177-ml. can frozen orange juice	6-fl. oz. can frozen orange juice
2 tablespoons orange liqueur	2 tablespoons orange liqueur	3 tablespoons orange liqueur
1 egg white	1 egg white	1 egg white

Put the sugar and water in a saucepan and heat until dissolved; leave to cool.

Meanwhile, in a cup, soak the gelatine in 2 tablespoons cold water then stand in a pan of hot water until dissolved. Stir the gelatine and undiluted orange juice into the cold syrup, mixing thoroughly.

Variation *Melon caprice*
Cut the top off a ripe melon and remove the seeds. Enclose in a polythene bag and chill in the refrigerator. When ready to serve fill the melon with

Pour into ice tray and freeze until mushy. Stir in the liqueur (Grand Marnier, Cointreau or other orange liqueur) and the stiffly whisked egg white, mixing evenly. Continue freezing until firm. Serve in shallow coupe glasses.

orange liqueur sorbet and serve on a bed of chipped ice.

Marsala ice cream

Serves: 4

IMPERIAL	METRIC	AMERICAN
3 egg yolks	3 egg yolks	3 egg yolks
3 oz. castor sugar	75 g. castor sugar	6 tablespoons sugar
6 tablespoons Marsala	6 tablespoons Marsala	$\frac{1}{2}$ cup Marsala
$\frac{1}{3}$ pint double cream	2 dl. double cream	scant 1 cup whipping cream
2 egg whites	2 egg whites	2 egg whites

Beat the egg yolks and sugar together in a large bowl until pale. Beat in the Marsala. Rest the bowl over a saucepan of near boiling water and, whisking vigorously all the time, beat until the mixture becomes thick and foamy, in about 5 to 6 minutes. Immediately remove from the heat and leave until cold, whisking

occasionally. When cold, add first the cream previously beaten until thick, and then the stiffly beaten egg whites – folding each in gently but thoroughly with a metal tablespoon. Turn into a small mould or basin, cover, and freeze until firm.

Quick ice cream coupes

When a rather special sweet is needed on the spur of the moment any of the following can be relied upon to create an impression. All you need is bought ice cream, and some fruit which you put to macerate in liqueur before you sit down for the first course. If available a swirl of whipped cream and/or a fancy wafer gives a finishing touch. Serve in individual glass dishes.

Coupe caprice
Sections of fresh orange soaked in Grand Marnier and topped with strawberry ice cream.

Coupe délice
Canned lichees just as they are but topped with Rum and citrus sorbet (see page 70).

Coupe félice
Diced honeydew melon laced with Crème de menthe and sugar to taste, and topped with vanilla ice cream.

Coupe fraisalia
Fresh strawberries sliced, sugared and flavoured with Kirsch, topped with vanilla ice cream and a small meringue shell.

Coupe jacques
Diced banana, strawberry and pineapple turned in lemon juice flavoured with Kirsch, topped with vanilla ice cream.

Coupe montmorency
Canned black cherries, preferably pitted, laced with cherry brandy, and topped with vanilla ice cream.

Tia Maria ice cream

Serves: 4

IMPERIAL	METRIC	AMERICAN
2 eggs, separated	2 eggs, separated	2 eggs, separated
2 oz. sifted icing sugar	50 g. sifted icing sugar	½ cup sifted confectioners' sugar
1–2 tablespoons coffee essence	1–2 tablespoons coffee essence	2–3 teaspoons instant coffee dissolved in 1–2 tablespoons water
2 tablespoons Tia Maria	2 tablespoons Tia Maria	3 tablespoons Tia Maria
¼ pint double cream	1½ dl. double cream	⅔ cup whipping cream

Whisk egg whites until very stiff, then whisk in icing sugar gradually. In another basin, whisk egg yolks, coffee essence and Tia Maria together, then whisk this gradually into the egg whites. Lightly whip the cream and fold into coffee mixture. Place in ice trays or a shallow tin, cover and freeze. There is no need to whip this ice cream during freezing. Serve with crisp biscuits.

Ginger cream split

Serves: 4

IMPERIAL	METRIC	AMERICAN
4 oz. gingernuts	100 g. gingernuts	¼ lb. (10–12) ginger snaps
2 tablespoons castor sugar	2 tablespoons castor sugar	3 tablespoons granulated sugar
2 tablespoons vegetable oil	2 tablespoons vegetable oil	3 tablespoons vegetable oil
1 egg white	1 egg white	1 egg white
¼ pint double cream	1½ dl. double cream	⅔ cup heavy cream
2 tablespoons brandy	2 tablespoons brandy	3 tablespoons brandy
2 teaspoons icing sugar	2 teaspoons icing sugar	2 teaspoons confectioners' sugar

Line an ice tray or small loaf tin with greaseproof paper. Put the gingernuts into a plastic bag and crush with a rolling pin. Mix the resulting crumbs with the sugar, and oil, and spread half the mixture evenly over the bottom of the tray.

Whisk the egg white until stiff. Whip the cream with the brandy until thick, then fold in the sugar and the beaten egg white. Pour into the tin, spreading evenly, and sprinkle the remaining crumb mixture over the top. Freeze until firm. To serve, turn out on to a flat plate, peel away the paper, and cut in slices.

Frosted liqueur mousses

Serves: 3–4

IMPERIAL	METRIC	AMERICAN
1 large egg white	1 large egg white	1 egg white
¼ pint double cream	1½ dl. double cream	⅔ cup heavy cream
2 tablespoons icing sugar	2 tablespoons icing sugar	3 tablespoons confectioners' sugar
2 tablespoons liqueur (see method)	2 tablespoons liqueur (see method)	3 tablespoons liqueur (see method)
1 oz. chopped toasted nuts	25 g. chopped toasted nuts	¼ cup chopped toasted nuts

Whisk egg white until stiff. In a separate basin whisk cream until beginning to thicken, then add sifted icing sugar and continue whipping until thick but not solid. Fold in egg white and liqueur (apricot brandy, Chartreuse, Grand Marnier, brandy or rum). Spoon into individual paper cases and sprinkle with nuts. Place in ice-making compartment and freeze until firm. Serve in the paper cases.

Rum and citrus sorbet

Serves: 4

IMPERIAL	METRIC	AMERICAN
4 oz. granulated sugar	100 g. granulated sugar	½ cup granulated sugar
½ pint water	3 dl. water	1¼ cups water
1 large lemon	1 large lemon	1 large lemon
1 orange	1 orange	1 orange
1 tablespoon rum	1 tablespoon rum	1 tablespoon rum
1 large egg white	1 large egg white	1 egg white

An exquisitely refreshing Escoffier-inspired ice. Put sugar and water into a small saucepan, heat gently until dissolved, then simmer steadily for 10 minutes. Remove from heat. Add thinly pared lemon rind, and leave to stand until *quite cold*. Add squeezed orange and lemon juices, then strain into an ice tray. Freeze until thick and mushy.

Now whisk white of egg until stiff. Turn the semi-frozen ice into a basin, add rum (no more than a tablespoonful) and whisk to mix thoroughly, then fold in stiffly beaten egg white. Return to ice tray and freeze until firm. Should the ice show signs of separating whilst freezing give it a good stir.

Glace Bénédictine

Serves: 4–6

IMPERIAL	METRIC	AMERICAN
3 egg yolks	3 egg yolks	3 egg yolks
3 oz. castor sugar	75 g. castor sugar	6 tablespoons granulated sugar
2–3 drops vanilla essence	2–3 drops vanilla essence	2–3 drops vanilla extract
½ pint milk	3 dl. milk	1¼ cups milk
¼ pint double cream	1½ dl. double cream	⅔ cup whipping cream
2½ tablespoons Bénédictine	2½ tablespoons Bénédictine	3 tablespoons Bénédictine

A lovely rich French custard cream ice, beautiful with Bénédictine, but experiment with other liqueurs as available. Put egg yolks, sugar and vanilla into the top half of a double boiler and beat with a wooden spoon until pale and creamy. Heat milk almost to boiling point then stir, by degrees, into the yolk mixture. Cook over near boiling water, stirring constantly, until custard thickens enough to coat the back of the spoon. Cool, stirring now and then.

When cold stir in the Bénédictine and the lightly whipped cream. Pour into chilled ice tray and freeze until firm.

Variations

Glace plombière
Chop 2 oz. candied fruits (pineapple, cherries, angelica, etc.), and soak in 2 tablespoons Kirsch or Cointreau for 1 hour. Fold into the ice when latter is semi-frozen, replacing the Bénédictine.

Glace Kirsch
Replace Bénédictine with Kirsch. A wonderful ice to serve with raspberries or strawberries.

Cakes, biscuits and gâteaux

Generally speaking it is a waste of good material to put wines or spirits into *raw* cake mixtures. Too much is lost during the baking process. Exceptions are rich fruit cakes where the dried fruits are allowed to imbibe the precious spirits overnight – the resulting plump and flavourful fruit really does produce a gorgeously moist and mellow cake that keeps and keeps.

In other cases you get better value by adding the wine *after* the cake is baked. Prick the surface closely with a *fine* skewer or darning needle and pour a little rum, brandy or sherry over, allowing it to seep through, before wrapping the cake and storing it away. This incidentally is a good 'rescue' device for a cake that has dried out through overbaking!

An excellent way of introducing special flavours to sponge and layer cakes is via the filling – butter cream, pastry cream or fresh dairy cream. Rum flavour carries well, so too do the concentrated flavours of liqueurs. Especially successful are the orange-flavoured liqueurs, coffee and chocolate flavours, Kirsch and the nut-flavoured Noyau.

Sicilian cream cheese sponge

Cooking time: 30–40 minutes
Temperature: 350°F., 180°C.,
Gas Mark 4
Serves: 6

IMPERIAL	METRIC	AMERICAN
sponge	*sponge*	*sponge*
3 oz. warmed castor sugar	85 g. warmed castor sugar	6 tablespoons warmed granulated sugar
3 large eggs	3 large eggs	3 eggs
3 oz. sifted self-raising flour	85 g. sifted self-raising flour	$\frac{3}{4}$ cup cake flour, sifted with $\frac{3}{4}$ teaspoon baking powder
filling	*filling*	*filling*
8 oz. cream cheese	225 g. cream cheese	1 cup cream cheese
3 tablespoons castor sugar	3 tablespoons castor sugar	$\frac{1}{4}$ cup granulated sugar
1 tablespoon marmalade	1 tablespoon marmalade	1 tablespoon marmalade
1 tablespoon orange liqueur	1 tablespoon orange liqueur	1 tablespoon orange liqueur
to assemble	*to assemble*	*to assemble*
3–4 tablespoons orange liqueur	3–4 tablespoons orange liqueur	$\frac{1}{4}$–$\frac{1}{3}$ cup orange liqueur
sifted icing sugar	sifted icing sugar	sifted confectioners' sugar

Preheat oven. Put sugar in mixing bowl and leave in oven whilst collecting ingredients. Line a 6-inch (15-cm.) cake tin with greaseproof paper, oil bottom and sides and dust with flour and castor sugar mixed. Add eggs to sugar and whisk steadily until mixture is mousse-like and thick enough to leave a raised trail on the surface when the whisk is lifted. Lightly and evenly fold in the flour and turn into prepared tin.

Bake in centre of preheated oven until well risen, golden and firm to the touch. Partially cool in tin before turning out on to a wire rack. When cold, if not required immediately, store in an airtight tin.

To make the filling, beat the cream cheese, sugar, marmalade and liqueur together until fluffy. (Some cream cheeses are softer than others and if necessary chill the filling for a while before using.) Split the cake horizontally into three and sprinkle each layer with one or more tablespoons of liqueur. Spread two layers thickly with the filling, then re-form the cake, pressing together lightly. Dust top and sides thickly with sifted icing sugar. Serve in slices, with pastry forks for eating. Excellent as a dessert or for a special tea-party.

Brandy snaps

(illustrated on page 63)

Cooking time: 7–8 minutes per tray
Temperature: 325°F., 170°C., Gas Mark 3
Makes: about 20

IMPERIAL	METRIC	AMERICAN
2 oz. golden syrup	50 g. golden syrup	3 tablespoons corn syrup
2 oz. butter	50 g. butter	$\frac{1}{4}$ cup butter
scant 2 oz. castor sugar	50 g. castor sugar	scant $\frac{1}{4}$ cup granulated sugar
scant 2 oz. plain flour	50 g. plain flour	scant $\frac{1}{2}$ cup all-purpose flour
1 teaspoon ginger	1 teaspoon ginger	1 teaspoon powdered ginger
1 teaspoon lemon juice	1 teaspoon lemon juice	1 teaspoon lemon juice
$\frac{1}{2}$ teaspoon finely grated lemon rind	$\frac{1}{2}$ teaspoon finely grated lemon rind	$\frac{1}{2}$ teaspoon finely grated lemon rind
$\frac{1}{4}$ pint double cream	$1\frac{1}{2}$ dl. double cream	$\frac{2}{3}$ cup whipping cream
1–2 tablespoons brandy	1–2 tablespoons brandy	1–2 tablespoons brandy

The original brandy snaps *did* contain brandy, but you get better value if you flavour the cream with brandy and put lemon juice in the wafers! Measure the syrup, butter and sugar straight into a small pan and dissolve over *low* heat. Off the heat beat in the sifted flour and ginger, lemon juice and rind. Drop 4 or 5 small teaspoons of mixture, well apart to allow for spreading, on to an oiled baking tray. Bake in centre of preheated oven, timing carefully, until lightly set and deep golden.

Remove from oven and leave for about 1 minute until firm enough to lift off the tray with a palette knife. Roll loosely around the handle of a wooden spoon, working quickly before the snaps become too brittle. Slide off the handle and cool on a wire rack. Repeat with the rest of the mixture. When cold, fill both ends with a little whipped cream flavoured with brandy.

Wine biscuits

Cooking time: 20–25 minutes
Temperature: 325°F., 170°C., Gas Mark 3

IMPERIAL	METRIC	AMERICAN
5 oz. plain flour	140 g. plain flour	$1\frac{1}{4}$ cups all-purpose flour
4 oz. butter	110 g. butter	$\frac{1}{2}$ cup butter
3 oz. castor sugar	85 g. castor sugar	6 tablespoons sugar
1 egg yolk	1 egg yolk	1 egg yolk
1 tablespoon sherry	1 tablespoon sherry	1 tablespoon sherry
1 egg white	1 egg white	1 egg white
finely chopped nuts	finely chopped nuts	finely chopped nuts

Sift the flour into a mixing bowl. Rub in the butter (which should be at room temperature) until the mixture resembles fine breadcrumbs. Stir in the sugar. Mix to a firm dough with the egg yolk lightly beaten with the sherry. On a lightly floured surface roll out thinly to about $\frac{1}{8}$ inch ($\frac{1}{4}$ cm.) thick, prick well and cut into a variety of shapes. Brush with lightly beaten egg white and sprinkle with chopped nuts. Transfer to baking sheet and bake in upper part of preheated oven, until cooked and golden brown. Cool on a wire rack.

Pastry cream filling

With a small wire whisk beat 2 egg yolks and 2 oz. castor sugar ($\frac{1}{4}$ cup, 50 g.) until pale and thick, then work in 1 oz. ($\frac{1}{4}$ cup, 25 g.) flour and 1 tablespoon milk. Bring remainder of $\frac{1}{2}$ pint milk ($1\frac{1}{4}$ cups, 3 dl.) to the boil, and whisk into egg mixture. Return all to pan and whisk until boiling, then cook 2 to 3 minutes, still whisking. Flavour to taste with 2–3 drops of vanilla essence and 1–2 tablespoons liqueur.

Raspberry and hazelnut torte

Cooking time: 15–20 minutes
Temperature: 375°F., 190°C.,
  Gas Mark 5
Serves: 6

IMPERIAL	METRIC	AMERICAN
5 oz. plain flour	140 g. plain flour	1¼ cups all-purpose flour
3 oz. butter	85 g. butter	6 tablespoons butter
3½ oz. castor sugar	100 g. castor sugar	7 tablespoons granulated sugar
2 oz. finely chopped hazelnuts	55 g. finely chopped hazelnuts	½ cup finely chopped hazelnuts
8 oz. raspberries	225 g. raspberries	1½ cups raspberries
½ pint double cream	3 dl. double cream	1¼ cups whipping cream
1–2 tablespoons Kirsch *or* Framboise	1–2 tablespoons Kirsch *or* Framboise	2–3 tablespoons Kirsch *or* Framboise

Sift the flour into a mixing bowl and rub in the butter until the mixture resembles fine breadcrumbs. Stir in 2 oz. of the sugar and the nuts, and knead into a stiff dough. Divide in half. Mark two 7-inch (18-cm.) circles on greaseproof paper-lined baking sheets, and with lightly floured knuckles press out the dough to fill the spaces. Neaten the edges. Bake in centre of preheated oven until golden brown. Cool.

To make up the gâteau, sprinkle raspberries (fresh or dry frozen) with remaining sugar and thaw if necessary. Whip cream until stiff and flavour to taste with Kirsch or Framboise. Spread two-thirds of the cream on one of the circles, top with most of the fruit and cover with second circle. Pipe remaining cream decoratively on top and stud with remaining raspberries. Good at tea-time or as a dessert.

Chocolate almond and rum gâteau

Cooking time: about 25 minutes
Oven temperature: 350°F.,
  180°C., Gas Mark 4
Serves: 8

IMPERIAL	METRIC	AMERICAN
4 oz. plain dessert chocolate	110 g. plain dessert chocolate	4 oz. semi-sweet chocolate
2 tablespoons rum	2 tablespoons rum	3 tablespoons rum
4 oz. butter	110 g. butter	½ cup butter
4 oz. castor sugar plus 1 tablespoon	110 g. castor sugar plus 1 tablespoon	½ cup firmly packed granulated sugar, plus 1 tablespoon
3 eggs, separated	3 eggs, separated	3 eggs, separated
2 oz. ground almonds	55 g. ground almonds	½ cup ground almonds
2 oz. plain flour, sifted	55 g. plain flour, sifted	½ cup sifted cake flour
icing and decoration	*icing and decoration*	*icing and decoration*
fine butter cream (see below)	fine butter cream (see below)	fine butter cream (see below)
1 oz. plain chocolate, melted	25 g. plain chocolate, melted	1 oz. semi-sweet chocolate, melted
1 tablespoon rum	1 tablespoon rum	1 tablespoon rum
few flaked almonds	few flaked almonds	few flaked almonds

A rich chocolate cake with a moist fudge-like texture. When cooked the centre should be slightly soft and underdone; if over-baked the fudge-like quality will be lost.

Line base of 8-inch (20-cm.) sandwich tin with greaseproof paper, grease and flour the sides. Break up chocolate and melt with rum in a small basin resting over a pan of near boiling water. When creamy remove from the heat. In a mixing bowl cream the butter and the sugar together until light and fluffy. Beat in the egg yolks one by one. In another basin whisk egg whites until stiff. Stir melted chocolate and then ground almonds into the creamed mixture. Carefully fold in alternately the egg white and flour making 3 additions of each. Turn into prepared tin and smooth to edges.

Bake in centre of oven for about 25 minutes, until firm around the rim but soft and slightly underdone in the centre. After cooling in tin for 10 to 15 minutes turn out carefully on to wire tray. When quite cold spread top and sides with butter cream flavoured with the melted chocolate and rum (see below). When firm decorate with flaked almonds.

Fine butter cream
3 oz. (85 g.) unsalted butter, slightly softened with 3 oz. (85 g.) sifted icing sugar (confectioners' sugar) and 1 egg yolk. When smooth and creamy beat in flavouring to taste (you can use 1 tablespoon rum, brandy or liqueur).

Drinks

Hot mulled wine in winter and cooling wine cups in summer are gay and friendly ways of offering hospitality. Relatively inexpensive too, and you will find many suitable wines under brand names in local stores.

Mulled wine

The one really important thing to remember is never allow the wine to boil, although it must be served very hot. Choose any inexpensive but sound red wine from any part of the world. Treat recipes as guides only and use more or less spice, sugar, lemon or other flavours to suit your own taste. The longer you infuse the drink the stronger the added flavours will become, so taste frequently and strain in good time. Fine glasses might crack under the heat so use inexpensive wine goblets, about 6 to 7 fl. oz. capacity. For a party, a punch bowl and ladle adds greatly to the festive atmosphere. The strength of a mull can always be increased by reducing the water or by adding more spirit or liqueur.

Dr. Johnson's choice

IMPERIAL	METRIC	AMERICAN
1 bottle red wine	1 bottle red wine	1 bottle red wine
12 lumps sugar, *or to taste*	12 lumps sugar, *or to taste*	12 lumps sugar, *or to taste*
6 cloves	6 cloves	6 cloves
1 pint boiling water	6 dl. boiling water	2½ cups boiling water
¼ pint Curaçao	1½ dl. Curaçao	⅔ cup Curaçao
¼ pint brandy (optional)	1½ dl. brandy (optional)	⅔ cup brandy (optional)
little grated nutmeg	little grated nutmeg	little grated nutmeg

A very old and popular mull of the eighteenth century. Put the wine, sugar and cloves into a saucepan and heat slowly almost to boiling point. Add the boiling water, the Curaçao, and brandy if used. Stir and taste, adding more sugar if you wish. Immediately pour into glasses and grate a sprinkling of nutmeg on top of each.

If for any reason this mull has to be kept warm, remove the cloves, otherwise their flavour may become too dominant.

The bishop

IMPERIAL	METRIC	AMERICAN
2 small lemons	2 small lemons	2 small lemons
6 cloves	6 cloves	6 cloves
2 oz. lump sugar	50 g. lump sugar	12 lumps sugar
1 bottle port	1 bottle port	1 bottle port
1 pint boiling water	6 dl. boiling water	2½ cups boiling water
pinch mixed spice	pinch mixed spice	pinch mixed spice

Another famous old English mull, very mellow and soothing. Wash and dry the lemons. Stick one lemon with the cloves and roast in a hot oven for 15 minutes. Rub some of the lump sugar over the skin of the remaining lemon to extract the zest. Put the port into a saucepan and bring nearly to boiling point. Remove from the heat. Add the boiling water, spice, all the sugar, the roasted lemon and half the juice of the fresh lemon. Infuse until the flavour is to your liking, then strain into a punch bowl.

Vin chaud

IMPERIAL	METRIC	AMERICAN
1 bottle red wine	1 bottle red wine	1 bottle red wine
2–3 tablespoons clear honey	2–3 tablespoons clear honey	3–4 tablespoons clear honey
good pinch cinnamon	good pinch cinnamon	good pinch cinnamon
1 orange	1 orange	1 orange
4–6 cloves	4–6 cloves	4–6 cloves
1 pint boiling water	6 dl. boiling water	2½ cups boiling water
2½ tablespoons brandy	2½ tablespoons brandy	3 tablespoons brandy

Put the wine, honey, cinnamon and the orange studded with cloves into a saucepan and heat *slowly* almost to boiling point, stirring now and then. Add the boiling water. Just before serving remove the orange and stir in the brandy.

Glühwein

IMPERIAL	METRIC	AMERICAN
½ pint hot water	3 dl. hot water	1¼ cups hot water
large pinch grated nutmeg	large pinch grated nutmeg	large pinch grated nutmeg
1 sprig mint	1 sprig mint	1 sprig mint
2-inch piece stick cinnamon	5-cm. piece stick cinnamon	2-inch piece stick cinnamon
2 tablespoons granulated sugar	2 tablespoons granulated sugar	3 tablespoons granulated sugar
finely pared rind and juice of 1 lemon	finely pared rind and juice of 1 lemon	finely pared rind and juice of 1 lemon
1 bottle red wine	1 bottle red wine	1 bottle red wine

This hot spiced wine is a favourite drink in the winter sports centres of Austria and Switzerland. Put *all* the ingredients except the wine into a saucepan and simmer for 15 minutes. Strain. Put the wine into the saucepan, add the flavoured water and heat thoroughly but *do not allow to boil.*

Wine cups

Refreshing and cool wine cups look very attractive and are often preferable to straight wine, especially for a group of people. The base can be an inexpensive medium or sweet white wine or a light red wine. The strength of the cup can be *increased* by starting off with less soda water, or *decreased* by adding more as the evening progresses. Fresh fruit is more refreshing and if you use canned fruit you may need to reduce the the sugar content. As with mulled wine, taste as you go, and adjust the recipe to suit the ingredients. Cups can be cooled by adding chilled wine and minerals or by adding ice – the latter will dilute the flavour, so plan accordingly.

Red wine cup

IMPERIAL	METRIC	AMERICAN
thinly pared rind of 1 lemon	thinly pared rind of 1 lemon	thinly pared rind of 1 lemon
icing sugar to taste	icing sugar to taste	confectioners' sugar to taste
scant ¼ pint medium sweet sherry	1 dl. medium sweet sherry	½ cup medium sweet sherry
1 bottle light red wine	1 bottle light red wine	1 bottle light red wine
little grated nutmeg	little grated nutmeg	little grated nutmeg
½ pint soda water	3 dl. soda water	1¼ cups soda water
thin slices peach, orange, and apple	thin slices peach, orange, and apple	thin slices peach, orange, and apple
sprigs of fresh mint and borage	sprigs of fresh mint and borage	sprigs of fresh mint and borage

Put lemon rind in a large jug, add sugar, sherry, wine and nutmeg and leave to infuse, in the refrigerator if possible, for 1 hour. Taste, and if liked add more sugar or a little orange-flavoured liqueur. Strain into a serving jug or bowl, add chilled soda water and decorate with fruit and herbs. Serve nicely chilled.

White wine cup

IMPERIAL	METRIC	AMERICAN
1 bottle Sauternes	1 bottle Sauternes	1 bottle Sauternes
4 tablespoons medium dry sherry	4 tablespoons medium dry sherry	$\frac{1}{3}$ cup medium dry sherry
4 tablespoons brandy	4 tablespoons brandy	$\frac{1}{3}$ cup brandy
scant $\frac{1}{2}$ pint pineapple juice	$\frac{1}{4}$ litre pineapple juice	1 cup pineapple juice
3 strips thinly pared lemon rind	3 strips thinly pared lemon rind	3 strips thinly pared lemon rind
1 tablespoon lemon juice	1 tablespoon lemon juice	1 tablespoon lemon juice
$\frac{1}{2}$ pint soda water	3 dl. soda water	$1\frac{1}{4}$ cups soda water
sprigs of borage and verbena	sprigs of borage and verbena	sprigs of borage and verbena

Put the wine, sherry, brandy, pineapple juice, and lemon rind and juice into a large jug. Cover, and chill for an hour. Shortly before serving add soda water and decorate with the herbs.

Gaelic coffee for one

Heat the glass thoroughly. Pour in 1 tablespoon of Irish whiskey and add 3 cubes of sugar, or more to taste. Fill goblet to within one inch of the brim with very hot black coffee. Stir to dissolve sugar. Top off to brim with fresh double cream poured gently into tilted glass so that it rests on top of the coffee. Do not stir. The charm lies in sipping the hot flavoured coffee through the cream.

Variations
Follow the method as above but in each of the variations substitute the appropriate liquor for the Irish whiskey:
Caribbean coffee: rum

Coffee Napoleon: brandy
Coffee balalaika: vodka
Highland coffee: Scotch whisky
Mexican coffee: Kahlua (coffee liqueur)

Brandy flip

Serves: 1

IMPERIAL	METRIC	AMERICAN
1 tablespoon brandy	1 tablespoon brandy	1 tablespoon brandy
$\frac{1}{4}$ pint cold milk	$1\frac{1}{2}$ dl. cold milk	$\frac{2}{3}$ cup cold milk
1 teaspoon sugar	1 teaspoon sugar	1 teaspoon sugar
1 egg white	1 egg white	1 egg white

Mix the brandy, milk and sugar together in a tumbler. Beat the egg white to a firm froth and stir lightly into the milk.

Hot milk punch

Serves 3–4

IMPERIAL	METRIC	AMERICAN
1 pint milk	6 dl. milk	$2\frac{1}{2}$ cups milk
2 oz. granulated sugar	50 g. granulated sugar	$\frac{1}{4}$ cup granulated sugar
2 drops almond essence	2 drops almond essence	2 drops almond extract
1 teaspoon finely grated orange rind	1 teaspoon finely grated orange rind	1 teaspoon finely grated orange rind
1 egg white	1 egg white	1 egg white
2 tablespoons rum	2 tablespoons rum	3 tablespoons rum
3 tablespoons brandy	3 tablespoons brandy	$\frac{1}{4}$ cup brandy

Put the milk, sugar, almond essence and orange rind into a saucepan. Bring just to the boil then remove from heat. Whisk the egg white to a stiff snow. Add to milk with the rum and brandy, whisking gently until the punch is frothy. Ladle into cups or heatproof glasses and serve immediately.

Cheese fondue party

For an informal gathering of family or friends a fondue party is extremely sociable. The requirements are so simple it can be organised at short notice, and at modest cost. Cooking presents no problem provided you have a suitable dish to make the fondue in. Best of all is the traditional Swiss 'caquelon', available in English stores. But any enamel-lined heatproof casserole will do, preferably not very deep. Make the fondue in the kitchen and then keep it gently bubbling over a spirit lamp in the centre of the party table. It takes only a few minutes to cook, so prepare the table and bread cubes first. A round or square table is ideal so that everyone can reach the fondue easily. Give each guest a long handled fork and a supply of 1-inch crusty bread cubes; pieces with crust are less likely to crumble in the fondue.

The technique is to spear a cube of bread, twist it in the fondue, then scoop it out coated with the creamy cheese mixture.

In Switzerland many forfeits are attached to losing a piece of bread in the fondue. A man must buy a bottle of wine or pay for the next fondue, while a woman must kiss all the men at the table!

A fondue can be a meal in itself, perhaps with a cold appetiser beforehand and salad and fruit to follow. Quantities given serve 4 for a meal or about 8 as a party dip. Drink a dry white wine with wine fondues, and cider with the cider version.

The Wine for making fondues

This is one of the few occasions when a really dry white wine is needed, preferably a light wine with a fairly high acid content. Swiss cheeses in particular melt more rapidly in an acid wine and lemon juice is often added to increase the acidity. Suitable wines are Neuchâtel, an Alsatian Sylvaner or a Moselle. A dry but too flavoursome wine can be mixed with water.

Swiss fondue

Cooking time: 5–8 minutes
Serves: 4

IMPERIAL	METRIC	AMERICAN
1 garlic clove	1 garlic clove	1 garlic clove
½ pint dry white wine	3 dl. dry white wine	1¼ cups dry white wine
2 teaspoons lemon juice	2 teaspoons lemon juice	2 teaspoons lemon juice
8 oz. Gruyère cheese, coarsely grated	225 g. Gruyère cheese, coarsely grated	2 cups coarsely grated Gruyère cheese
8 oz. Emmenthal cheese, coarsely grated	225 g. Emmenthal cheese, coarsely grated	2 cups coarsely grated Emmenthal cheese
1 tablespoon cornflour	1 tablespoon cornflour	1 tablespoon cornstarch
2 tablespoons Kirsch	2 tablespoons Kirsch	3 tablespoons Kirsch
pepper, nutmeg *or* paprika to season	pepper, nutmeg *or* paprika to season	pepper, nutmeg *or* paprika to season

A typical Swiss fondue of which there are many local varieties. Rub the base and sides of a heatproof casserole with the cut clove of garlic. Pour in the wine and lemon juice and place over a gentle heat. When the wine is warm but not hot add the cheese gradually, stirring all the time. Bring almost to the boil, by which time the cheese will have melted.

Blend the cornflour with the Kirsch and stir into the fondue, with seasoning to taste.

Allow to bubble gently, stirring continuously for 1 to 2 minutes. Transfer to a spirit stove where it can continue to bubble very, very gently. If, towards the end, the fondue becomes too thick, stir in a little wine or milk.

Cheese and wine fondue

Cooking time: 5–6 minutes
Serves: 4

IMPERIAL	METRIC	AMERICAN
1 garlic clove	1 garlic clove	1 garlic clove
½ pint dry white wine	3 dl. dry white wine	1¼ cups dry white wine
1 lb. mild Cheddar cheese, coarsely grated	450 g. mild Cheddar cheese, coarsely grated	1 lb. mild Cheddar cheese, coarsely grated
3 teaspoons cornflour	3 teaspoons cornflour	3 teaspoons cornstarch
salt, pepper, and nutmeg to season	salt, pepper, and nutmeg to season	salt, pepper, and nutmeg to season
1–2 tablespoons Kirsch (optional)	1–2 tablespoons Kirsch (optional)	1–3 tablespoons Kirsch (optional)

Rub the base and sides of a heatproof casserole with the cut clove of garlic. Pour in the wine reserving 2 tablespoons for blending the cornflour. Toss in the grated cheese and heating *gently* and stirring continuously, bring the mixture to just below boiling point when the cheese will have melted. Blend the cornflour with the reserved wine and stir into the fondue with the Kirsch if used. Season to taste and allow to cook gently for a minute or two. Transfer to spirit lamp or plate warmer, and keep warm. The mixture should be of a coating consistency and will thicken as it cools.

Cheddar and cider fondue

Cooking time: 5–6 minutes
Serves: 4

IMPERIAL	METRIC	AMERICAN
1 garlic clove (optional)	1 garlic clove (optional)	1 garlic clove (optional)
little butter	little butter	little butter
½ pint dry or medium cider	3 dl. dry or medium cider	1¼ cups dry or medium cider
1 lb. mild Cheddar cheese, grated	450 g. mild Cheddar cheese, grated	4 cups grated mild Cheddar cheese
2 tablespoons cornflour	2 tablespoons cornflour	3 tablespoons cornstarch
pinch cayenne, salt and nutmeg	pinch cayenne, salt and nutmeg	pinch cayenne, salt and nutmeg

Rub the cut clove of garlic around base and sides of a medium sized saucepan, and then lightly butter the pan. Reserve 2 tablespoons of the cider, and pour the rest into prepared saucepan. Heat cider gently until it just begins to steam. Add cheese, about a tablespoon at a time, stirring in each addition until it melts before adding the next. Blend cornflour with the 2 tablespoons cider, and stir into cheese mixture. Season to taste, remembering that cayenne is very hot. Stir over heat for a further few minutes until mixture is almost boiling, then turn into fondue dish and place over gentle heat. Serve with squares of toast or bread for dipping.

Index